Zoo Goofs

Kristin Hilton

Ranting Raven Publishing
www.zoogoofsbook.com
info@zoogoofsbook.com

Kristin Hilton

Zoo Goofs

True Tales of Zookeeper Misadventures

Kristin Hilton

Library of Congress Control # 2011915576

Hilton, Kristin Anne
Zoo goofs: true tales of zookeeper misadventures/Kristin Hilton

ISBN # 978-0-615-51858-9 (paperback)

This is a work of nonfiction based on the experiences of the author. However, names, places, physical descriptions, and other particulars have been changed. For that reason, readers are cautioned that some details in the text may not correspond to real people, places, or events.

Book design by: Sara Curtis and Harriet Simpson; Advisor: Tom Fillebrown/Sierra College
Front cover photo: Red-breasted toucan chicks four weeks old by Kristin Hilton
Spine art: Cheetah by Alex Hilton, age 5
Back cover photos: Feeding great hornbill by Dick George
                   Week-old red-breasted toucan nestlings by Kristin Hilton

Published by: RANTING RAVEN PUBLISHING
              Meadow Vista, CA
Visit: http://www.zoogoofsbook.com
Email: info@zoogoofsbook.com

DICK GEORGE

DICK GEORGE

Honest, the keeper's not trying to strangle this owlet! It's just that he hatched only moments ago and can barely hold his oversized head up.

DICK GEORGE

For a nest cavity, an oak wine barrel is about the only "tree hollow" able to stand up to the massive beaks of these hyacinth macaws.

Contents

Contents

Contents

DICK HILTON

KRISTIN HILTON

Sometimes a giant anteater's baby hitches a ride on the mother's back.

A helmeted guinea contemplates the loss of one of his feathers. The original inspiration for the term "pinhead?"

Dedication

This book is lovingly dedicated to:

Imelda, Weasel, Buddha, Jason, Coco, and Bossy, and all the zoo animals that enriched my life immeasurably—only the overflowing treasure chest of cherished memories eases the heartache of missing all of you;

The precious memory of my mother, Aileen, who inspired me with her love of books and nature;

And especially to my husband, Dick, for giving me the opportunity to love and share the life of a truly brilliant and passionate man. You have only an inkling of the depth of my respect and devotion.

Acknowledgments

There was rarely a day that I didn't eagerly look forward to working at the zoo. The animal keepers I had the privilege of working with over an eighteen-year career have been the most dedicated and professional people one could ever hope to work alongside. Their capabilities were surpassed only by their sense of compassion. They were also a whole lot of fun.

May I say, too, that the success of any zoo's animal department unquestionably depends on the dedication and support of all the other departments that round out a zoo, such as maintenance, horticulture, concessions, administration, security, etc. The animals and their keepers may tend to get all the attention, but it is truly a cooperative effort.

Over the years of putting this book together I have relived old memories and revived forgotten ones when talking to old friends. With all that comes a new appreciation of my good fortune in amassing such unique relationships and experiences. What an incredible foundation to have built my life on!

I would like to express more thanks than is possible to the following people that helped make this book a reality:

All my former coworkers (I wish I could name you individually but the people and locations in the book are anonymous!);

"Sister" Susie Haeffner, so sensitive and caring, who keeps me in stitches;

Long-time friend Marsha McGrath for early encouragement and helpful suggestions;

Sister Janice for diligently helping find errors on numerous drafts and her husband Rich Scandalis for being a good sport;

Brother John Buhl for his inspiring quiet manner and attention to detail;

Son Brad, competent computer wiz, for all his patient rescues, and his fabulous family Brenda, Josh, Zach and Alex;

Son Jake, sagacious and personable, for letting me be your wicked stepmother, and his affable wife Kelly and son Parker;

Dependable, erudite friend Robert Haungs;

Photographer extraordinaire Dick George, for capturing and generously sharing so many fond memories in an endowment to last a lifetime. The book is decidedly richer with all your superb photos;

Sierra College Professor Tom Fillebrown for hooking me up with personable and patient graphic design students Sara Curtis and Harriet Simpson, and for putting up with my excess of enthusiasm;

A particular expression of gratitude to Sara Curtis, for sharing her gift for design, computer abilities and calm demeanor;

And to the many others who didn't know what they were getting into when they gave so generously of their time, including: Suzanne Villareal, Pat Antuzzi, Geri Stout, Patricia Saulsbury, John-Michael Keating, Ron Claridge, Mike Hendrix, Casey Lantz and Marjorie Heckman.

DICK GEORGE

Keepers and marabou stork have a chat.

RICK HAEFFNER

Hand-raising chicks like this crowned crane creates a unique bond between keeper and bird; it's what makes all that poop raking worthwhile.

Preface

You might think it strange that I chose a career as a zookeeper for I believe that exotic animals make totally inappropriate pets, and in a perfect world none should live in captivity at all. But I justify zoos when looking at a discouraging broader picture.

I am struck with pessimism when I see how our precious planet is plagued with overly fecund humans who are gobbling up land and resources at a disastrous rate. In our greed we are destroying habitats at an unprecedented rate. The arrogant attitude toward nature that so many fellow humans seem to have baffles me. Can it be attributed to the lack of knowledge and impressionable experiences that should be acquired in one's youth?

"Virtual reality" education in classrooms is now the substitute for field trips. How can you really learn about a tide pool without feeling sticky saltwater dry on your skin after plucking a seastar from a rock? Or running your hand over a convoluted rock outcropping, wondering How did that happen and how long did it take? How do you endure desert heat while piquant creosote fumes pierce your nostrils—in a classroom? They don't even take field trips to the local zoo. Truly sad. It is such a genuine problem in today's world that a specific term has been coined for it: Nature Deficit Disorder.

It is amazing to me how seldom people travel to different regions of the United States, let alone global adventures. My husband teaches at a college a mere 2-hour drive from the coast, yet every semester a show of hands reveals numerous students who, incredibly, have never laid eyes on the ocean! This generation is growing up thinking the real world consists of malls, highways, and subdivisions. They experience "Nature" by mowing a lawn or spending the morning on a golf course (let's not even get started on those subjects!). "Wildlife" is some unidentifiable blob flattened on the road.

Nature programs on television can enlighten us only so much. There is nothing like engaging your senses in real wildlife experiences such as when the pungent odor of elephants hits you in the nose on a sultry summer day; the raucous squawks of a flock of busy parrots drown out all other sounds; or you feel the roar of a lion resonate deep in your stomach.

It's easy to become exasperated by today's worrisome concerns such as the economy, and overpopulation (control *that* one and *all* other problems are diminished). You may not be able to go to the jungles of Brazil or the African savannah, but why not escape to nature by spending a leisurely day at a zoo? Not everyone can afford to travel the world, nor should they. So I justify zoos as an essential tool to help teach youngsters an appreciation of nature and an escape for adults. People need to see and hear exotic animals and, if the zoo does it right, get an idea of what their habitats resemble.

Few things enriched my life more than the varied travels I have taken over the years. Besides seeing most of the US including Hawaii and Alaska, I have gone on nature tours in Africa, Central and South America, Baja, and Australia. There is just no education or adventure like it. I grew up in the northeast US with a passion for animals and plants and yearned to see the world. I moved to the southwest to attend college and got a degree in horti-culture, intending to become a landscape architect or nursery owner.

The US economy was suffering a recession at that time making it virtu-ally impossible to find a job (in desperation I showed up at a local Pizza Hut for an advertised waitress position and found some thirty other appli-cants milling about). An odd moment in the college library during my last semester, however, changed the course of my life. You could often find me rummaging through the nature section of the stacks for a good animal or natural history book to read. That day I happened across a set of books titled *The International Zoo Yearbook.* In the first volume that I pulled out, and on the first page that I opened to, was an article about a community college in the southeast that had a small teaching zoo on the campus. Ah, serendipity! What better alternative to choose than to continue my education? I spent the next nine months at that college, cleaning and helping build exhibits while blissfully enrolled in fascinating animal husbandry courses.

I wanted to work with big cats, but at this zoo the largest feline they ex-hibited was a margay. And besides that, about every three weeks everyone rotated his or her assignments. During my last month at that school we were choosing our final assignments and no one would volunteer for the "chickens, ducks, geese, turkey, and peafowl" category. I finally spoke up, saying I would take them on the condition that I could also have the brown pelicans. Deal. And what a deal it was. The pelicans had built a nest for

KRISTIN HILTON

the first time and were incubating three eggs, and during my watch all three of them hatched. The zoo director said that pelicans almost never raise more than two chicks, and that I should take the last one to hatch home and hand raise it. That did it. From then on I was hooked on birds.

The next fifteen years found me back in the southwest, working at a young zoo—an oasis of nature surreally surrounded by a bustling big city. I gradually learned just how complex bird behaviors and husbandry are, and how comparatively boring (as my opinion grew) mammals seem. With some 8,000 different species in the world, birds are an extraordinary challenge to learn about, but oh, so rewarding.

At one point during my zoo career I took a four-month leave of absence to work on an endangered species project on the big island of Hawaii. My main assignment was to hand-raise chicks from a pair of critically endangered Hawaiian crows held in the state's captive breeding facility. Then a two-year stint at a tiny, old zoo in a small town in the northwest US followed before I retired from zoo work altogether. Geez, what a fantastical career!

Today's zoos bear little resemblance to the original miserable collections of animals known as *menageries* that date back hundreds of years. Back then, because exotic wild animals were uncommon, difficult to collect, and challenging to properly maintain, they became status symbols that only royalty or the wealthy could afford. At times the curiosities were brutally pitted against each other, their natural behaviors exploited for ghoulish amusement. Some collections became traveling shows to entertain commoners. A modern-day royal menagerie in the Middle East held the critically endangered Arabian oryx for private pleasure and exclusive hunting. Ironically, that small herd was to become the key to the survival of the species (see: the "Oryx Interactions" chapter).

In stark contrast, modern zoos are sophisticated and dedicated institutions of education, conservation, research, and medicine. And many stand at the forefront of global conservation issues, making that all-important difference. Thankfully, too, times have changed enormously since I amassed these stories with regard to safety and communication. The younger generation will undoubtedly find it hard to fathom, but please bear in mind when reading the book that my early years as a keeper occurred before we had radio communication or telephones in exhibits (let alone cell phones). Please try to avoid being judgmental as hindsight is always clearer and I've deliberately chosen stories that don't reflect the norm. As I said, zoos have made incredible strides in safety and professionalism.

I am honored and proud to have witnessed recent transformations of zoos and participated in my own very small way as an animal keeper and bird curator. I hope the following stories impart to you a taste of how special the life of a zookeeper can be. Over the years I have been approached by countless enthusiastic youngsters saying how much they love animals and would love to have my job—What's it really like? Perhaps reading this book may provide some inspiration to the next generation of idealistic keepers.

Brown pelican nestling.

DICK GEORGE

A rare opportunity to release a captive bird back into the wild.
To learn about this Harris hawk see the last story in the "Tiny Tidbits"
chapter.

A zookeeper's job helps build strong muscles and stamina.

Introduction

Mostly, it's the same routine day after day for an animal keeper, opening and closing countless exhibit doors, gates and locks. You have to stick to a routine or something can be forgotten. Endless raking and hosing become robotic, and you find yourself musing on the distinctive odor of lake algae steeping in the hot sun, the effusive vocalizations of grackles, or the sight of two monstrous giraffes as they bash their long necks against each other. Your senses magically transport you to foreign lands. But then there is a sudden hesitation, a gut feeling that jolts you back to reality. You can't be sure: Did I really lock that gate or not? Should I go back and check?

Considering that zoo workers are continually exposed to potential danger their safety records are stellar. Keepers are an extremely cautious bunch, constantly working with a heightened sense of attentiveness. They have to. Accidents can occur due to distractions or when laziness tempers good judgment. At other times things may be beyond your control such as a poor decision by a zoo visitor. Even though the animals are in a captive situation they can retain some of their wild heritage—which may be unexpectedly revealed at any time. Keepers can get lulled into a false sense of trust when nothing significant happens, until one day....

It's rare, but an animal keeper may find himself in an unforeseen episode of terror, comedy, or tragedy—you just never know what might happen when you start your morning at the zoo. Each workday brings an element of novelty, unlike any that an accountant, waitress, or shoe salesman could ever imagine in their jobs.

The following stories are based on true incidents, with the names of all the individuals and animals changed, and the zoo locations unidentified.

WARNING: Some of the stories may not be suitable for sensitive readers or young children.

To stimulate a crowned pigeon chick to eat when hand-feeding, keepers mimic the feel of the parent's beak by slipping our fingers in an inverted V-shape over the chick's beak. The parent regurgitates food to him--we use an eye dropper.

These "pinfeathers" are deeply engorged with blood, nourishing the developing feather. It may seem contrary to logic, but plucking out an accidentally broken pinfeather that steadily drips is the best way to prevent serious blood loss.

A Brief Encounter

O h wow, thought Kyle, she's cute! I like the way her long blonde ponytail bounces alluringly on those bare shoulders. She looks so cool and fresh even though it's so darned hot out. And it looks like she's here at the zoo all by herself.

The petite little blonde in her bright yellow sundress caught the zookeeper's eye as she strolled through his work area of the big cats, rhinos and great apes. Tall and twig-thin with a thick mop of black hair, Kyle just happened to be between girlfriends. He hoped for a chance to meet her, and kept just ahead of the blonde's wanderings so he could secretly observe her from the indoor parts of the exhibits (known as night houses). Anticipating her next move, he soon came up with a clever idea. He could grab a bucket of bananas and grapes at the next exhibit and really impress her by hand-feeding the two young orangutans that were housed there. Then he'd have an excuse to strike up a conversation.

While the girl watched the massive rhinos munch their hay, Kyle trotted from that exhibit over to the orang night house and pulled the fruit from the refrigerator. Peeking out the window, he could see when she approached the railing outside the apes' exhibit. The keeper stepped outside, shoved his unruly hair out of his eyes, and began divulging all the neat stuff he knew about the animals to her.

"Aren't these animals something else? Did you know that wild orangutans live in rainforests on the islands of Borneo and Sumatra?" he asked as he broke off hunks of banana to offer the two animals. "And in the Malay language, orangutan means 'person of the forest.'" He admitted to her that sometimes it's a bit unnerving to make eye contact with them at such close range.

"It's weird," he joked, "it's almost like there's really a person in a furry suit looking back at you." To draw out the interaction time with her, he passed one slice of apple at a time to the apes.

She seemed genuinely interested in what he talked about, so Kyle prattled on. "They're only about 4 to 5 feet tall but they're massively built primates, with big bulky adult males weighing maybe 200 lbs. Have you seen the father of these two yet? He's just enormous and really intimidating! Because they spend most of their lives moving about up in trees they develop these mighty arm muscles, you know, with arms about twice the length of the legs. Look at their feet, too; they look more like hands—with opposable big toes, like thumbs, for gripping branches, see?

"And let me show you this really cool thing we do with them." While chatting away, he showed her how the keepers would often empty out their pants and shirt pockets and stuff them with hard-boiled eggs, grapes, nuts, and other goodies. "We hide all their favorites in our pockets and stand close to let the orangs discover and fish out the treats. It feels kinda creepy to have their fingers rummaging around right next to your body.

"Of all the zoo's animals," Kyle said, "my favorite ones to work with are these two guys, 'Rosie' and 'Frodo.' They were both born here, and are 5 and 7 years old right now. If they were human kids, they'd be like rambunctious teenagers—mischievous, you know? But not vicious, and boy what a lot of fun to play with."

As the captivated blonde watched him interact with the orange-haired apes, Kyle flashed a big smile at her. Blinking demurely when she smiled back at him, he noticed the cute dimples in her cheeks. Rosie and Frodo reached through the bars of their exhibit, rifling through Kyle's bulging pockets like they normally did. The blonde's rapt attention at all this made the keeper feel absolutely giddy.

"It's really sad though," he told her. "This species is critically endangered because of poaching and humans destroying their habitat. Some experts predict they'll be extinct in the wild maybe in just the next couple of decades. It's such an awesome opportunity for us keepers to be able to work with such rare, unique primates, but man, what a big responsibility, too.

Engrossed in flirting and showing off his knowledge, he failed to notice that the apes had soon emptied his pockets of the treats. Two impatient hands began pulling at them. Pretty soon four hands jerked at his clothes. Then there were four hands and two feet mashing Kyle up against the bars. And now it was too late. Before he could react, he had four hands and four feet tugging and tearing his clothes and biting off his shirt buttons. Impatient for more goodies and screeching with exhilaration at this new element of the game, the orangutans gripped Kyle so tightly that he couldn't break away. They weren't being aggressive so much as caught up in a frenzy of excitement.

Rosie just flat out grabbed the keeper's khaki pants, abruptly yanking them over his slim hips down to his knees. He stood stunned and helpless

CINDY BARRY

in his underpants and ripped shirt, still pinned against the bars. Then in one quick motion Frodo reached through the bars, seized Kyle's exposed briefs, and whisk!, tore them right off! Frodo always wanted to wear things like palm fronds and banana peels on his head, so of course he bounded away while pulling Kyle's underpants over his head down to his ears. Peering through one of the shredded leg holes, he jubilantly swung on the exhibit branches and ropes to show off his prize. Right in front of the blonde.

With Frodo gone, Kyle managed to break free from

Rosie's grip. He gathered what was left of his tattered shirt about him and averted his eyes, embarrassed to watch as Frodo flaunted his painfully acquired underpants. He focused his eyes on the floor while struggling to pull up the ripped khakis. Kyle couldn't bear to see those deepening dimples as the blonde undoubtedly laughed at his involuntary exposure. Grabbing his jacket from the hook on the door, he fumbled to tie it around his skinny waist to hold up his pants. Then he sprinted to the back of the zoo and slipped into his car, racing home to change his clothes. He hoped to return to work before anyone noticed he was gone.

Kyle had been told one time that he had an unusually cute butt, but he didn't dare stick around to find out if the cute little blonde had been impressed or not.

A Simple Misstep

My introduction to just how dangerous an animal keeper's job can potentially be occurred when I attended a college with a small zoo on its campus. Each student got first-hand experience caring for a wide variety of animals while attending classes pertinent to becoming a professional keeper.

The zoo maintained a group of five black-handed spider monkeys. In the wild, these endearing primates live in small troops in Central and South American tropical rainforests. Weighing only about 20 lbs., the generally passive and good-natured spider monkey is constantly on the move. His yard-long prehensile tail exceeds the length of his body, and comes in ever so handy as a fifth limb. The last ten inches or so of the tail's underside is really unique in that it lacks hair, and is covered instead with leathery skin that resembles the sole of a barefoot hiker. The monkey has elongated fingers and toes, but surprisingly, no thumbs. Almost totally arboreal with long and lean "spidery" arms, legs and tail, the monkey flaunts perfect grace and agility as he brachiates through the branches of high tree canopies.

Back then the zoo's spider monkey exhibit was an enormous but boring cage with a concrete floor, lots of branches, and a few ropes to swing on and not much else. (Costly plans for a new, heavily landscaped display were on hold indefinitely until the sizable sum of money could be raised.) Built into one corner of the cage, a cozy night house with lots of hay bedding provided shelter for the monkeys to nestle in at night and during inclement weather. The keeper, Karen, could close the night house door to lock the animals safely inside while she worked in the exhibit. At least that was the plan. But trying to shift these lively monkeys from the exhibit into their night house always failed. As soon as two or three went in and an exasperated Karen finally encouraged the others to cooperate, the first ones darted right back out, and

so on. It may as well have been a revolving door. So to save time and not stress the monkeys, the keeper always cleaned the exhibit with the animals present.

One morning, as usual Karen hosed the cage floor as the monkeys clambered about the branches and swung on the ropes. She occasionally glanced up to keep track of all five monkeys' whereabouts. Deep in thought about something other than her chore, she blankly watched the stream of water spray against the concrete as she moved about. Then Karen took a step backwards. A catastrophic step backwards. Not realizing that the male spider monkey was scrambling about on the floor right behind her, she unintentionally stepped on his long toes.

After some thirty years, I still cringe when I recall that scream of agony as the monkey's sharp canines sank into the back of Karen's ankle, severing her Achilles' tendon. For a long six months after that excruciating encounter she wore a cast and hobbled about on crutches while it slowly healed. I can't even imagine the emotional trauma she must have suffered.

This incident obviously caused the keeper horrendous pain, but it was purely accidental and not malicious on the part of the spider monkey. And

HARRIET SIMPSON

at Karen's expense, all of us other students learned the valuable lesson of needing to always stay attentive when working with animals.

I still remember my first incident of personal bodily harm with remarkable clarity, and how amazed I was at how quickly the unexpected can happen. Fortunately it was a very mild lesson, and more importantly, I didn't cause any animals or fellow keepers to be injured.

The zoo's three rheas (named "Pyorrhea," "Gonorrhea," and "Diarrhea" by some demented keeper) needed to be loaded into a trailer to move them into their new exhibit. Five-foot tall birds (and thankfully flightless), rheas are South America's more demure version of the African ostrich. A rhea's maneuvers to elude a predator would make even the most agile quarterback trying to evade burly tacklers jealous. With each turn, running in a crazed zigzag pattern, a rhea flails his neck and wildly waves the large fan-like wings from side to side to create confusion as to which direction he is really headed.

Being new to zoo work, I have to admit I had never even seen a rhea before. It felt weird to stand right next to her, and be looking eye-to-eye. John and I hadn't really discussed what the plan entailed, but he knew exactly what he was doing. In one quick motion, he grabbed the bird from behind by the wings and adeptly pinned Pyorrhea between his thighs. He intended to simply fast-walk the bird through the gate and up the ramp into the waiting trailer, which he neglected to tell me. Once John had hold of the 60-lb. bird I thought surely I should be of some kind of help to him and stepped forward, but didn't really know what to do. The protesting rhea vigorously lashed out with her feet, and so of course with me stupidly standing right in front of her I got an abrupt and painful kick in the leg. Fortunately my pant leg afforded some protection, but to this day I still have the nice pea-sized divot that Pyorrhea's toenail removed from my shin to remind me that all I was expected to do was close the trailer tailgate behind the bird. From then on, whenever possible, I made sure I understood the game plan before dealing with any critters.

Warthogs often inhabit empty aardvark dens, typically *backing* in to use those intimidating tusks to guard the entrance.

Oryx Interactions

Ah, the majestic oryx of Africa with those trademark horns and elongated faces with striking color patterns. Oryx wield their long, ribbed horns as a defense against predators and during sparring to establish dominance within the herd. Some species' horns are sword-blade straight, but others, like those of the scimitar-horned oryx, sweep back in a graceful curve. Male oryx are particularly aggressive, maintaining their harem against rival suitors. Beisa oryx, one of the larger varieties, stand an imposing 6 feet long and over 4 feet tall at the shoulder, and their beefy bodies weigh up to 400 lbs. Their ebony horns measure an astonishing 4 feet long.

A legendary, rather gory story often circulated among zookeepers told of a crusty old Texas rancher who kept a variety of exotic animals on his property including several different species of oryx. Walter exemplified the classic sinewy cowboy, clad in tight jeans, Stetson hat, and well-worn boots. Early one morning he stopped his pickup truck at the gate to the 20-acre section of scrubby land where a herd of some twenty beisa oryx roamed about. Being a particularly stubborn man, good judgment sometimes took a backseat to his arrogant attitude. For some foolish reason, on this day he decided to walk out to the animals' nearby waterhole. He dropped the tailgate down so his devoted old coonhound could hop out and plod along with him. After they had hiked in a ways, Walter cussed aloud when the aggressive oryx bull suddenly appeared on top of a low hill in the distance, and then just as suddenly disappeared from view. At that point, the reckless rancher realized he had better head back in the direction of the truck and picked up his pace. Beads of nervous sweat trickled down his back. Just where was that crafty animal now? Meanwhile the oryx circled around through the scrub-covered hills, somehow always managing to keep out of sight. Then, without the rancher even seeing him coming, the oryx ambushed him from behind.

A rapier-sharp horn pierced into the back of Walter's thigh, through his groin, and poked out the other side of his leg. The agonizing puncture ripped open his femoral artery. The rancher's knees collapsed, but he couldn't fall to the ground with the ribbed horn firmly stuck in his leg. With an abrupt toss of his head that wily beast then pitched the old man up in the air like he was

no more than an annoying piece of brush caught on his horn. Walter landed hard on his back, so hard that he couldn't draw a breath without excruciating pain. The oryx continued to lunge and stab at him as he writhed on the ground. That rancher was as tough as a strand of barbed wire but no match for the unre-

Beisa oryx

lenting oryx, who ignored the harsh clouts in the face Walter wielded with his Stetson. Walter wrapped his arms over his chest and rolled away behind a bush, then managed to stagger to his feet and frantically wave his arms, shouting at the oryx in an attempt to scare it off. As the dog joined in the fracas its incessant baying and cavorting aggravated the crazed oryx. During the distraction the man managed to inch himself up into a nearby scraggly old mesquite tree, which put him just high enough to evade those deadly horns. On the brink of shock, he then fashioned his shirt into a tourniquet to control his leg's spurting blood vessel.

If his persistent hound hadn't finally chased away the oryx the rancher might have bled to death. He later said that neither broken ribs, the goring, nor the struggle to make the painful hike back to the truck was even the worst part. It happened when the emergency room doctors reamed out the throbbing wound with a big long swab soaked with nerve-electrifying antiseptic.

The smaller Arabian oryx are just about the size of our deer. Dwelling in the desert, their strikingly white coat vividly contrasts their brownish-black and white face markings. In winter, the hair on their legs grows in darker to absorb the sun's warmth. Adorned with horns that measure nearly the length of a yardstick, this species of oryx weighs up to 160 lbs. Due to poaching they number less than a thousand in the wild. The zoo maintains about one hundred of them in an enclosure of several acres, sectioned off to hold separate groups of breeders and bachelor herds.

Tall, hefty, and a bit bandy-legged, Jack was the most senior of all the keepers. His beguiling, omnipresent smile complemented his even-tempered disposition. Which was amazing considering he suffered chronically sore knees swollen to the size of cantaloupes; they had kept him from being drafted into the Army in the 1960s. For years, doctors told him he was the perfect candidate for artificial knees but I guess he figured he'd rather live with the debilitating pain than go under the knife. Jack had a quirky behavior too, of being overly cautious about locks. He would repeatedly tug on a padlock or jiggle the handle of a locked door to be certain that it was indeed secured. He even admitted to instances when he would be on his way home and would turn around to drive back to the zoo to check a particular lock just one more time.

Jack had worked at the zoo from its inception, literally helping build it while he learned about the animals. He told many tales of those early days, like before the convenience of simple plumbing—of lugging water in big white buckets long distances to the various enclosures every single day.

After hearing of the Texas rancher's gruesome experience over coffee at morning break a few days before, Jack was busy raking in the pens that held the zoo's collection of precious Arabian oryx. While tuning in to the rhythmic scratching of his rake on the hardpan of the paddock, he pondered what terror that man must have experienced. Meanwhile the keeper kept a close watch on the herd leader, "Clint," a particularly bellicose old male.

The fine weather on that Sunday morning had brought a sizable number of visitors to the zoo. After answering a patron's numerous questions, which caused a considerable crowd to gather, the keeper resumed raking while scanning the herd for Clint…who was now nowhere to be seen. Jack took a step or two back so he could get a look along the side of the barn and cringed in horror when all of a sudden he felt the imperative jab of Clint's horn at the back of his thigh. I can't believe it, he thought, this is the rancher's nightmare, but it's happening to me!

In a death-defying move, Jack whirled around to face Clint with the only thing he could use for defense—the bamboo rake. Striving to keep his balance on those troublesome knees, in sheer panic he wildly flailed away with the flimsy rake to drive off his attacker. Just as quickly though, Jack realized that it wasn't Clint who had poked him after all. His relief instantly crumbled

into mortification, however, on the further realization that this large crowd of people just w i t n e s s e d him fiercely thrashing the handle of the *wheelbarrow!*

After he considered the story of the gored rancher though, easy-going Jack couldn't help

A rare Arabian oryx, pregnant with a precious contribution to the next generation.

CINDY BARRY

but smile, pleased that he'd had that reflex in case the wheelbarrow had actually been feisty old Clint.

Clint was such a strong, belligerent animal that one day he managed to pull a keeper right off his feet. As with the usual plan when moving oryx, Rich grabbed hold of Clint's horns from the other side of the stall panel (which stood 4 feet high). But the powerful oryx wrenched his head away while backing up, pulling the 6-foot 3-inch-tall keeper along with him. Determined not to let go, Rich found himself dragged over the barrier to his waist, then thighs, then beyond the point of return. Fortunately Jack happened to be nearby and grabbed Rich by the ankles, hauling him back over the partition before the keeper ended up right in the close confines of the stall with that nasty Clint.

KRISTIN HILTON

The size of a tennis ball, an adult African black crake has black plumage, orange legs, red eyes and an outrageous chartreuse beak. As small as they are, crakes are surprisingly aggressive during breeding season (which may occur year-round).

Humpty Dumpty at the Zoo

Only about 6 inches long, an African black crake is a handsome, jet-black bird with red eyes, chartreuse beak, and orange legs. Its ridiculously oversized feet are perfect for pattering across lily pads. A bit on the hyperactive side, these demure little creatures scurry about, poking in the water and vegetation for bugs and seeds.

After completing my keeper routine at the end of a pleasant spring day I found I had a little extra time before heading back to the commissary where I would clean up some dirty dishes, replenish supplies for the next day, fill out my daily keeper report, and then leave for home. I decided to use those few moments to install some exhibit modifications that seemed like they might encourage our shy new pair of crakes to reproduce. I cut some nice big fresh palm fronds and leaned them against the mesh in a kind of tilted A-frame in a couple of locations in their exhibit. I hoped these would act as privacy shelters for the birds. The very next day they busied themselves with building a dainty grass nest between one of the sets of fronds. And within a short two weeks the crakes had the nest filled with five pointy beige eggs profusely speckled with flecks of brown and orange. They certainly hadn't wasted any time, and I felt satisfied that I'd stumbled on an innovative idea for the crakes to readily utilize.

Both the male and female shared the nesting duties for nearly all of the 22-day incubation period. But a day or two before the anticipated hatching of the eggs I noticed that neither crake was brooding on the nest. Thinking maybe I had miscalculated the date I anxiously took a quick peek to see if there were any new little chicks. Five precious eggs still sat in the darkness of the palm frond shelter, and—how thrilling! It appeared one was hatching! But on looking a little closer, I saw that the egg didn't have the usual "pip" cracks on the big end that a hatching chick makes from the inside with its "egg tooth." This egg had apparently been tampered with by one of the adults.

I guess these novice parents had lost patience, and whatever possessed them to do it we can only speculate. But I will never forget the awful sight. The egg was intact except for two small holes toward the pointed end. And to my dismay, out of each of these holes a parent had somehow managed to pull out the dead chick's limp orange legs. It was sickening, but the egg looked a lot like a perfect little Humpty Dumpty.

All five of the eggs contained fully developed, but dead, chicks. We suspect that the eggs failed to hatch when they became chilled after the parents' premature abandonment. There is a happy ending to the crakes' rather morbid story, though. Future nest attempts have been quite successful. In fact, they have become surprisingly prolific and attentive parents, every year raising two or more clutches, each with four or five young. A crake chick is an adorable little pompom of black fuzz smaller than a ping pong ball, carried around on lanky stick legs with sprawling feet that dwarf the little body.

Everyone knows that baby animals can cause zoo visitation to skyrocket, especially with popular animals like pandas or tigers. It is just as exciting for zookeepers when any of the animals we work with every day reproduce. Although first attempts may not always be successful, both the animals and staff learn significant lessons with each successive endeavor.

Crakes may not draw a big crowd of zoo visitors, but they are pretty unique little birds that hold a special spot in my heart. And thankfully, there have been no further incidents of Humpty Dumpty eggs at the zoo.

The egg tooth on the tip of the beak of this newly hatched African black crake chick hasn't fallen off yet.

DICK HILTON

The spirals adorning the crowned crane's head resemble strands of untwisted golden wire. The white patch is naked skin as soft as kid leather, and the black forehead looks like a fuzzy pompom of short, compact feathers.

On the Job Training

The big day had finally arrived. And what a perfect day it was—bright and sunny with a cool temperature and persistent light breeze. This was Abby's first time working solo after a week of intense training by her coworkers. She had always dreamed of someday working at the zoo she visited so often while growing up and now here she was. During her last year of college she had worked part time for a veterinarian, but this job marked the start of a new career and she couldn't be more excited. A little intimidated too, with all the responsibility, but it was all just so thrilling.

Abby wore her shiny black hair pulled back into a perky little ponytail. As thin and lithe as a gazelle, she scampered about while preparing for the day's chores. As part of the job routine, she loaded all the supplies into the rowboat and paddled her way out to "Spider Monkey Island" where a troop of six spider monkeys lived.

One of the monkeys, ancient "Old Sue," was a true senior citizen in spider monkey years and liked to walk alongside the keepers during their visits. She could be a little bit loony, sometimes doing unpredictable things. Like one time she was seen in the water quite a few feet off the island, with her spindly arms held high over her head as she gingerly waded up to her armpits. Apparently she intended to retrieve something she had spotted bobbing in the water. We consider this unusual behavior because many primates usually won't even venture into the water. They don't know how to swim, which makes an island a perfect display option. The zoo has several islands in its lakes that display other primates too, such as gibbons, squirrel monkeys and tamarins. No mesh, bars or other barriers means unimpeded viewing for the public, albeit at a long distance from shore to island.

Anyway, back to Abby's activities. It took only about 15 or 20 minutes for the new keeper to work through her various chores. First she distributed the monkey biscuits and nuts to the metal feeder bins and emptied the buckets of chopped fruits and vegetables in several locations. Then Abby pulled the old hay bedding out of the big night box, a large structure for the monkeys to sleep in or escape inclement weather. She dumped the big bag of fresh hay she had brought along into the box and fluffed it around. With the bag now empty, she slipped the old hay into it and raked up the previous day's orange and banana peels and other "leavings."

Engrossed in her work, thinking everything through to make sure she didn't forget anything, it took Abby a while to notice that Old Sue hadn't been shadowing her. And, hmm, none of the monkeys were digging through the piles of fruits. In fact, where were the monkeys? Something wasn't right. Abby began to feel a little sick to her stomach. She quickly gathered up the buckets and hay bag to put back into the boat so she could investigate the mystery.

Standing there on the shore with her arms laden with stuff Abby looked around for the boat. Where the heck was it? Dumbfounded, it slowly dawned on her that the rowboat no longer sat at the edge of the island where she'd left it. Poor Abby dumped everything on the ground. Then she noticed that there, way off in the distance, was the boat floating out of reach, about fifty feet off shore. That was troubling enough, but now she could see that *all six of the spider monkeys were sitting in the boat* as it bobbed about in the water! They all sat rigid and frozen facing the bow, staring wide-eyed straight ahead. Each had its tail and long fingers clamped tight on the rim of the boat. But their appearance seemed more one of expectation—like they were just anxiously waiting for the tardy gondolier to arrive. And there, poised regally in the front of the boat, sat Old Sue showing great equanimity.

Another keeper, Ben, just happened to drive by along the lakeshore when he saw Abby waving to him. He smiled and gave a nonchalant wave back and was continuing to drive off when her gestures became more exuberant. She started jumping up and down, frantically waving both arms over her head. Once Ben stopped the cart he could hear her distant pleas for help.

After assessing the situation Ben yelled his idea to her across the water, then sped off and found another keeper to help load up a boat from one of the zoo's other lakes. It seemed to Abby that the rescuers were never going to return while she helplessly watched the boatful of monkeys floating perilously farther away. And what about that nice lilting breeze she had found so

pleasant before? Now she detested how it encouraged the boat to drift ever closer to the mainland. Tears came pouring down her cheeks as she thought of what a disaster the day was turning out to be. Over and over, for the long, endless time she had to endure the wait, all she could think was, I'm going to be fired. I've tried to be so careful to do everything just right and look what I did. I'm going to lose my job. I haven't even made it through the first day, and I'm going to be fired.

The two keepers arrived with the rescue boat just barely in time to nudge the drifting boat of perplexed passengers safely back to their island. As the shore came in reach the monkeys all scampered off, fleeing to the tops of the trees where they stayed the rest of the morning. Abby had incredible luck that the boat hadn't floated any nearer to the mainland and all six monkeys gone on the loose. How ever would they have caught them back up? She didn't know if she felt more relieved or the monkeys did.

It sure wasn't the way she'd pictured the start of her new profession. But at least there were no further consequences. In most serious incidents like this a keeper could be fired or suspended depending on the circumstances and outcome. Because she was new and nothing more serious ended up happening that day, the curator decided she had suffered punishment enough. From then on Abby made sure to tie the boat to one of the trees on the island. And you can pretty much bet that those brash seafaring spider monkeys never desired to get anywhere near that boat again, except maybe Old Sue (who from then on we called Sailor Sue).

Striding majestically across the savannah, when a secretarybird encounters a snake—a favorite prey item—he "punches" it repeatedly with balled up foot.

Lucky Lazy Lisa

am so glad to have worked mostly with birds during my 18-year zoo career. I found them infinitely diverse in behaviors and husbandry, and thus more challenging than mammals. Also, relatively few birds pose any real danger to work around. Because of the potential for catastrophe, apprehension always overshadowed my confidence any time we were short-handed and I'd have to work with the great apes, elephants, or big felines. Whenever I did, as I went through the routine I would constantly check and re-check the doors and locks, and glance about to be sure the transfer doors were still tightly closed (and that the animals sat on the other side of those doors from me!). I still shudder whenever I recall a dramatic incident when Lisa, the keeper for the big cats, worked in the exhibit housing the African lions and Bengal tigers and *she* ended up on display instead of the lions.

The busiest part of the workday for keepers is early morning, getting everything ready before the public comes through the zoo entrance gates. So usually everyone is preoccupied with chores and somewhat isolated in their own work area for several hours. I don't know how long Lisa must have sat out in the exhibit that memorable morning before help finally came along, but it had to be at least two long, nerve-wracking hours.

At many animal exhibits, a "keeper safety" system of two doors separated by a vestibule ensures an added layer of security (there is always a closed door to keep an animal from getting out while the keeper enters or exits). A keeper locks and unlocks so many doors, padlocks, and gates throughout each workday that it can become rote. He might get preoccupied, and then assume that he must have secured that crucial door or gate latch. Sometimes he can get overly confident, in a hurry, or just cavalier, and deliberately leave doors or gates open. Laziness can tempt a careless keeper to foolishly skip that extra protective measure. What happened the day of the episode involved a series of incidents of poor judgment peppered with laziness.

The lion and tiger outdoor exhibits flank either side of the building with the night quarters inside. After Lisa finished cleaning the lions' exhibit and pond, she passed through the keeper door into the night house hallway. Intending to go back out to turn off the water filling the pond, she left the door open. Once she rounded the corner, however, she got distracted fussing with something else. A little later on, with the still-open keeper door out of view, she slid open the male lion's transfer door letting him out from the night house to the exhibit. As usual, "Samburu" ambled outside. But then, woops! promptly re-entered through the open keeper door, right into the hallway with Lisa.

She was lucky that day, for Lisa happened to be standing by a gate she had left wide open. She slammed it shut, dropped the latch and backed away just as Samburu caught sight of her. It was a rather flimsy gate, not meant to be a regular barrier between keeper and cat, but at least it offered some degree of protection (although more psychological than real). Samburu, a confident and placid adult, weighed in at a hefty 550 lbs. and measured nearly 8 feet long, not including his tail.

Lisa was also lucky because even though he would occasionally snarl at you Samburu was very mellow. Without fail, the female lion, "Mbili," feigned an "attack" on her keeper while waiting to be let outside, which was pretty intimidating considering her body wasn't that much smaller than the male's. She would rise up on her muscular hind legs, towering over the keeper on the other side of the chain link mesh. The belligerent lioness clawed at the mesh while fiercely roaring and exposing those deadly canines. Standing just inches from her gaping mouth and feeling that blast of hot breath in your face evoked primal fear; the throaty roar resonated in your ears and stomach. She seemed to take special pride in this provocative

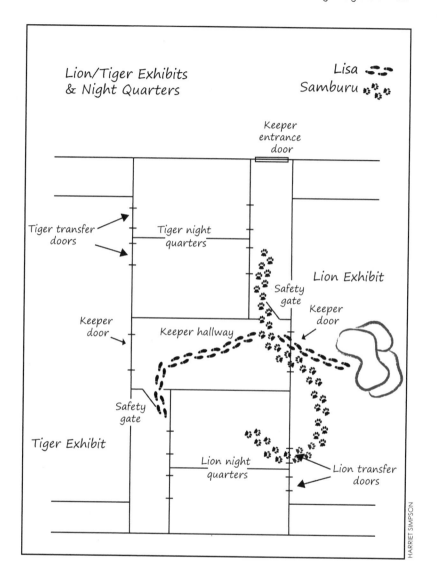

Lion/Tiger Exhibits & Night Quarters

Lisa

Samburu

Keeper entrance door

Tiger transfer doors

Tiger night quarters

Lion Exhibit

Safety gate

Keeper door

Keeper door

Keeper hallway

Safety gate

Tiger Exhibit

Lion night quarters

Lion transfer doors

HARRIET SIMPSON

game. Even though you knew Mbili waited in ambush to pull that snarling bluff every single morning, it always hit you deep in the gut. If it had been that brat Mbili in the hallway instead of serene Samburu, without hesitation she would certainly have charged the inadequate gate, and at a solid 400 lbs., probably broken through.

With even more incredible luck that day, Samburu turned and headed down to the opposite end of the long hallway to check out the adjoining tigers' quarters. Up until now, the lions and tigers could only hear and smell each other; they had never been eye-to-eye ever before. Excitedly flicking his tail as he swaggered down the hall Samburu bumped his hip against another safety gate Lisa had left open, which swung partially closed behind him. Trembling uncontrollably, the keeper bravely snuck behind the preoccupied

lion, pulled the gate closed and flipped down the latch. As she leaned against the wall, with weak knees she slid to the floor in relief. But then she made a horrifying realization: That particular hallway where the lion now stood also led to the building's entrance door. The only door. Lisa's only way out of the lion/tiger exhibit.

This incident happened many years ago, before keepers had radios or cell phones. Because she couldn't leave through the building door, Lisa's only option was to lock her self outside "on display." The exhibit design incorporated a deep, dry moat that the animals couldn't scale, so of course Lisa was unable to climb out either. She perched anxiously on one of the immense granite boulders in the middle of the exhibit that the lions enjoyed sprawling on in the mid-day sun. When the first zoo visitor finally strolled by, Lisa anxiously explained her predicament. Then she had to wait for that person to roam about the grounds to locate another employee. Once word spread, a rescue group quickly formed to discuss their limited options. Getting the lion secured and Lisa safely out of the situation took another hour or so of some complicated finagling that rather anticlimactically went without incident. But Lisa could never look back on this event without an odd mix of feelings of fear, relief, and embarrassment.

But that wasn't quite the end of the story for her. Depending on the severity of the situation, reprimands for negligence by a zookeeper can result in a letter in the employee's personnel file and possibly suspension for a day or more. A blatantly remiss, potentially deadly situation involving dangerous animals like this one could rightfully cause a keeper to be fired, especially if there was a dubious history of incidents. Depending on the circumstances, episodes like this not only endanger the life of the zookeeper but possibly those of coworkers, the public, and the animal as well.

Lisa's lucky streak held, and for some reason the curator decided on only a letter of reprimand in her file and a week's suspension without pay. The whole experience undoubtedly revised lazy Lisa's propensity to leave night house gates and doors open.

ZACH HILTON, AGE 10

Magnificently colorful sunbirds are the Old World version of our hummingbird.

A Life-Changing Experience

P aul was a big, burly guy with short legs and a barrel chest. His fine, thinning blonde hair matched the light sprinkling of wispy whiskers barely visible on his upper lip. He currently worked in the birds section of the zoo and wanted to eventually learn all the different keeper jobs. He had a peculiar habit during the morning work break, which keepers usually spent together at one of the zoo's snack bars. Every day, Paul bought the biggest carton of popcorn available and dumped it all out on the picnic table. He then spread it in a single layer with his stubby, fat fingers and slowly ate one kernel at a time. Over his popcorn one morning, Paul told Jack, the oryx keeper, that he wanted to learn the capture technique for the Arabian oryx. He'd never had the opportunity to work with them before and just wanted to get some experience interacting with them.

In their native desert habitat on the Arabian Peninsula oryx have been the victims of poachers. Their numbers plummeted in the 1940s with the advent of automatic weapons and Jeeps. By 1972 the noble animals were extinct in the wild. Fortunately, however, a few precious individuals survived in privately owned herds, most notably on sprawling estates of Middle Eastern royal families. Today Arabian oryx are one of only a handful of endangered species success stories. Aggressive captive breeding programs initiated in 1962 led to numerous reintroductions as early as 1982 into protected wild

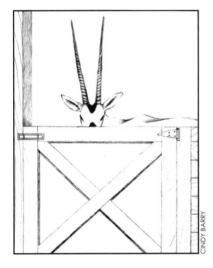

areas in Oman (which adjoins Saudi Arabia and Yemen), with varying degrees of success. (For more information check out oryxoman. com and the many other web sites regarding the fascinating oryx.)

Thorough records kept on most animals at zoos pay particular attention to bloodlines. Population management decisions to avoid inbreeding and maximize genetic diversity sometimes dictate the shifting of individuals between enclosures or to other zoos. One day one of the oryx needed to be moved from one pen to another, so Jack arranged for Paul to help him. The plan was to catch one of the aged females, load her into a trailer, and release her into a pen with a herd of other non-breeders. Jack thoroughly briefed Paul on every detail. Once the trailer was in place and they were ready to begin, Paul reached over the stall partition of the barn and grabbed hold of one of the old oryx's horns right next to her head, just as Jack had instructed him to do. That way he could control her head and those fierce black horns, while his body stayed hidden safely from hers behind the stall panel.

The moment the startled oryx felt the keeper grip her horn, she wrenched her head around and with a dry, brittle "crack!" the horn broke off in Paul's hand. It snapped off at the base, just like that! Paul stood there, dumbfounded, with his pudgy fingers wrapped around the horn of this incredibly valuable endangered species.

It turned out that her horn was paper thin at the base. She was so old and had worn it down so much from frequent rubbing that it just snapped off. Jack reassured Paul that it was really no big deal for her, especially because there was no bleeding. In the wild and at a zoo oryx horns can sometimes break when they spar against each other, which they do all the time.

Jack said he thought Paul had felt so distraught that he later went on to be a curator at a museum somewhere. A place with no live animals.

Ride 'em Cowboy

The early morning sun already sizzled with white-hot, glaring heat, promising a brutal day to be working outdoors. Just another in a string of days with cruel, record-breaking temperatures. You had to avoid sitting on a sun-drenched bench in this weather, lest your buns get toasted. A bunch of wilted keepers later sprawled around the snack bar picnic tables at lunch break, sipping icy drinks and trying to make it through the last couple of sweltering hours of work. A couple of them were new on the job and hadn't heard all the old timers' famous zoo stories yet. In an attempt to get their minds off the stifling weather, Jack mentioned that Rich had been involved in a lot of adventures over the years. He encouraged Rich to relate one of his most notorious tales, the New Year's Day rhino incident. Tall and slim with curly black hair and a thick tangle of beard, Rich was a confident, mellow kind of guy that was just a delight to be around. He also told great stories.

Rich said that he remembered every detail like it happened yesterday. "New Year's Day is one of the busiest days for numbers of visitors at the zoo," he said. "It was ten years ago, and the skies were that gorgeous clear blue you get with nippy weather, you know? And throngs of visitors just packed the zoo trails. I'll tell you what happened from the beginning from my point of view. It turns out some other things had gone on that day that I didn't know about, but this is how it all happened for me.

"I was in the night house of the gorilla exhibit and we were keeping the male inside; he seemed to have a cold and we had the television on for him. (The female gorilla's favorite program was *Star Trek.*) It was late in the day and I had my work done, so I popped into the night house to see who was winning the Rose Bowl on the TV. While I flipped through the channels, all of a sudden I heard this really loud pounding on the door. When I opened it, there was this kid who worked at the snack bar, jumping up and down and flapping his arms. He was all pale and sweaty. He started yelling at me, 'Hurry, hurry up, the rhino is gonna kill him!'

"I stepped outside away from the TV noise and said, 'What?'

"He shouted, 'If you don't hurry and do something quick the rhino's gonna kill this guy.'

"And I still couldn't figure it out. 'What are you talking about? What guy?'

"The kid screamed, 'Somebody is *in* the rhino exhibit!'

"Well at that, I slammed the door and locked it, and then ran like I've never run before. Man, I was flyin'. When I made it to the rhino exhibit it looked like a football stadium with hundreds of spectators! There must've been 500 people standing there all around the exhibit, and more were running from all directions. I could see a crumpled body laying in a heap on the ground in the exhibit and I thought, Oh, man. What're we gonna do? This is before we had any kind of communications, too. No phones in the night houses, no radios to carry with us, and no cell phones.

"So I hurried into the rhino's night quarters and threw some sweet feed down in the holding pens. I slid open the transfer door and jingled my keys, calling their names. Even though it was hours earlier than normal for them to come in, the two rhinos, it was "Mubu" and "Hashi" at the time, came strolling inside just like usual when I bring them in for the night. And then it hit me. I thought, Okay, I got the rhinos away from the guy, but now there's hundreds of people waiting for somebody to do something. And that somebody is me! What the hell am I going to do?!

"I figured this guy's probably in shock if he's alive, so I'd need to cover him up. I went running out there with this big canvas tarp that I found in the night house. I was going to cover him to keep him warm, compress any bleeding and all that stuff, you know? So I ran out and looked at this guy and he was perfectly motionless. I couldn't see any breathing and there was blood on his clothes but it didn't look like a huge amount. But I'd never seen a body contorted that badly before. And I thought, A body that is bent in that many different directions cannot possibly be alive. Especially one that's not moving or breathing.

"Right at that moment as I'm thinking all this, a priest holding a little red leather book jumps down off the wall into the exhibit with me and starts mumbling something over him. I couldn't believe it. It just didn't seem real. And I thought, Oh no, this guy really is dead! I mean I wasn't sure, I hadn't taken that close a look, but he must be dead if the priest is doing that.

"Well, I covered him up completely with the tarp so the people wouldn't see his dead body. Lying a few feet away was something—what was it? It turned out to be a straw cowboy hat the man must've been wearing, squashed flat as a flour tortilla by one of the rhinos. Then next to it, half buried in thick mud, I noticed what looked like the top half of a shoe. Then, finally, I felt so relieved when Kyle came speeding up on his cart. He was the first other keeper on the scene and I sent him for help, to call for an ambulance. After he left, it was like, how long is all this taking? Thirty seconds? Four minutes? Ten? The priest and I kept giving each other these solemn looks and didn't know what to do but just stand there. All I know is I was terrified and had no concept of time except that it just seemed to drag on forever. Just then I heard this real low moan," Rich said, "and the tarp starts to move, so I thought, Ooh, better give this guy some air!

"Kyle returned to see what else he could do to help. It seemed like an eternity passed, and the ambulance still hadn't shown up, so I sent Kyle

KRISTIN HILTON

back to the security office to check on it. As it turned out, right before I got there another guy had tried to help the hurt person, the 'cowboy,' get out of the exhibit, and he'd gotten hurt himself. He tried to be a Good Samaritan, and he got gored in the crotch. He jumped in because the cowboy was unconscious and laying face down in a mud hole. It had rained the night before, and he thought the guy might suffocate in the mud.

"The Samaritan hefted the cowboy onto his shoulders, but the mud in the puddle came up to his ankles and it sucked his shoe off. He slipped and fell to his knees, and that's when the male rhino came up and bopped him from behind. As the guy's body pitched forward he lost his grip on the cowboy. But worse yet, he was injured himself. Mubu's big thick horn had gone between the man's legs, and when the rhino lurched his head up the point of his horn ripped open the man's scrotum. One of his testicles dangled out by the sperm cord. The Samaritan stood up, kind of tucked his testicle back in his pants, and then scrambled over the wall to get back out of the rhino exhibit. Then, you know—he was probably in shock—he walked all the way through the zoo to the entrance and parking lot, and somehow drove himself to the hospital.

"But, meanwhile, what happened was, by the time he managed to get to the front of the zoo, word had already hit the security office that somebody was hurt in the rhino exhibit and to call an ambulance. Then they saw the Samaritan walk out with blood-soaked, torn pants so everybody knew he'd been hurt, but he refused to let anyone help him. They thought that since the guy drove himself to the hospital they should call back and cancel the request for the ambulance.

"So when Kyle went back to the entrance to find out what the delay was, they said, 'No, you cancelled it.' And Kyle said, 'No, I didn't. We need that. We *need* an ambulance, NOW!'

"Of course, when it did finally come, the ambulance went to an obscure gate in the zoo's perimeter fence, one that hadn't been used in years. This gate had such an old padlock on it that none of the security guards had the right key. And so after even more of this delay the ambulance had to drive clear around to a different perimeter gate.

"It's interesting what you find out a day later. Where the story starts from my point of view with the rhino there's only the cowboy. And I don't know why the ambulance is taking so damn long. I remember the next day the curator called me in to his office. He wanted to hear what had happened from my perspective, and then he told me about the Samaritan. When he told me about the guy's testicle hanging out I remember thinking how excruciating it must've been, and subconsciously covered my crotch with my hands. Just when I was doing that, one of the secretaries happened to walk by the doorway and asked, 'Hey, whatcha got in your hands there, Rich?!'

"And I realized I looked kinda stupid standing there holding my balls, but I thought I was only subconsciously holding them while hearing about that poor Samaritan.

"The rhino exhibit had been divided in half with barricades—you know, those big concrete ones like they use on the highway. These kept the rhinos away from where their big service gate at the far end was being replaced. The cowboy who had jumped into the exhibit that day was apparently pretty rip-roaring drunk. He'd decided to do a rodeo ride on a rhino. Mubu bounced him off those barriers like he was in a handball court—like he was playing handball, with the cowboy as the ball. The poor guy ended up in the hospital in traction and with numerous casts, but at least he survived.

"We heard that when the Samaritan found out that the cowboy had been drunk and deliberately leapt onto the rhino's back he said if he had known that he never would have tried to save him. He assumed he had fallen in.

Rich continued, "I heard that, before he jumped in, the cowboy was heard yelling, 'There ain't no rhino cain't be rode, there ain't no cowboy cain't be throwed....'"

The feathers of a newly hatched ostrich look more like stiff slivers of woody fibers. Weighing about 3 pounds, one ostrich egg equals around 24 chicken eggs.

Don't Ever Volunteer

The outdoor exhibits for the zoo's African lions and Bengal tigers flank the same night house. The building consists of indoor chain link enclosures to keep the big cats in their own quarters for the night. This separation capability is also helpful during unusual situations like a birth, medical problem, or introduction of new animals. The cats always eagerly come inside from their exhibits when the "evening keeper" feeds them. (An evening keeper drives around in a pickup truck or golf cart, patrolling the zoo grounds after the keepers have left for the day. He delivers final feedings, gives medications, and shifts certain animals into their night quarters once the zoo closes.) In the morning after the day keeper finishes readying the outside exhibits the animals go back out on display. Then he safely cleans the indoor quarters at a later time.

Rich and Kyle shared an apartment while they attended college and worked together as zookeepers. One afternoon, Kyle was supposed to work the evening keeper shift but needed some extra study time for a big biology exam coming up the next morning. Rich had the day off, so he generously volunteered to fill in for him. He could use the extra money anyway.

Absolutely exhausted, Rich stumbled through the apartment door at ten o'clock that night, about two hours late for coming home from the evening keeper job. Kyle was still studying at the desk when Rich plunked himself down in the armchair, blinked at Kyle, and with total exasperation related that evening's incredible drama.

It was already getting dark as Rich pulled up in the pickup truck to the lion/tiger exhibit, his last stop. When the keeper opened the night house door and traipsed down the hallway carrying the cats' buckets of meat he thought he heard this muffled moaning that sounded vaguely like, "Help me, help me." But he couldn't be sure. He couldn't tell where it was coming from. Startled, he stopped and leaned forward, eager to hear, but—nothing but silence.

"Cal" was a big male tiger, weighing some 450 lbs. and he waited outside in the exhibit by himself. The zoo was keeping Cal and his mate, "Meru," separated because she had recently given birth to three cubs. She was lying inside waiting for her dinner while the babies contentedly nursed from her. Maybe that weird sound came from one of the cubs, he thought, and continued on with his chores. First Rich fed Meru. Then he slid Cal's meat from the bucket into the feeding pan and pulled the handle to open the sliding transfer door (part of the regular routine to get the big cats to come inside for the night). But Cal didn't come rushing in as he usually did. The keeper jingled his keys while calling the cat and, instead of the tiger, a *man* popped his head in through the door. The guy looked young, probably in his early twenties, and had an expression on his face unlike any Rich had ever seen.

The empty bucket dropped from Rich's hand, clanging to the floor as he ran out of the building and around to the exhibit. Ohh, this is some serious trouble, he thought. And sure enough, there on the other side of the door he saw that the tiger had hold of the guy by the leg. But rather than mauling the man, Cal seemed to be playing with him, like he was a big toy. It took a moment for the surreal scene to register and for the keeper to collect his thoughts. Rich ran back to the entrance hallway where a rifle was stored in a cabinet for just such rare emergencies, which thankfully had never happened before. But none of his keys fit the lock. His heart pounded so hard he could feel it in his ears. He was panicky, and now totally frustrated. So without hesitation Rich grabbed a shovel and smashed the glass to access the rifle. Then he hurried outside, wading into the thick, waist-high bushes at the edge of the exhibit. Reluctant to shoot the weapon, first he tried yelling, waving his arms and clapping to distract the tiger, but to no avail.

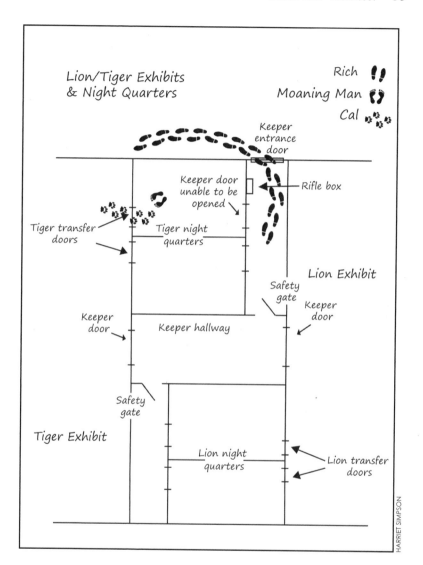

The trouble then, was, no one had ever shown him how to use this particular rifle, a .30-06. He had used others in practice shooting before, but never this one. Rich cocked it, but each time he did the shells kept ejecting. He would put the weapon up to his shoulder and fire at Cal, but nothing happened, and he kept loading the shells back in. Much as he hated to have to do it, in this life and death situation Rich felt obligated to shoot the tiger.

Trying to fire at silhouettes, though, with only the eerie light of a just-rising full moon, he feared he might hit the man instead of the tiger. But the rifle wouldn't work. If he could just fire into the dirt to make enough noise to scare Cal into leaving the guy alone…but he couldn't get the rifle to do even that. He would close his eyes and squeeze the trigger, but it kept jamming.

Rich looked up from his struggles with the rifle in time to notice that this poor, agonized man was somehow managing to drag himself through the tiger's cat-sized narrow transfer door. Rich dashed back inside, yelling encouragement to the man, "Hurry, you can do it!" Meanwhile he kept slowly pushing the door ever more shut to exclude Cal. Then, at just the right moment, he quickly slid the lever to slam the door shut, leaving the tiger outside and the man safely inside. What a relief!

Crisis over, right? Hardly. Rich took one look at the man and had to grab onto the bars as his knees buckled. Pretty much all the skin and muscle was gone off the guy's left leg from the knee down to his ankle. There was just bloodstained bone and a growing puddle of blood on the floor under his knee. I gotta get this guy to a hospital, Rich told himself. But as he reached for his keys to open the padlock, he found that in all the turmoil somehow they didn't get clipped back onto his belt loop. He had lost his keys, so now he couldn't open the door to pull the man out of the tiger's night quarters. Rich finally had him away from the tiger, but still couldn't get to him!

Well, at about this time, a patrolling security guard happened to come along. He didn't have the key they needed either, but did have a loaded pistol. So cowboy-style, he tried to blow the padlock off the latch of the mesh door. But, unlike in the old westerns, it didn't work. With an ear-piercing ricochet the bullet flew wildly across the hall. They decided it was obviously much too dangerous to keep trying that. Time was crucial for this piteous man who lay limp and clearly in shock, and Rich desperately tried to think of more options. Briefly, he pictured himself as a cartoon character with all these silly bubbles of thoughts floating over his head. What should I do next?

With the headlight beams bouncing wildly, the security guard raced his golf cart down the bumpy shortcut path to the zoo entrance to call for an ambulance. Meanwhile Rich sped off in the truck over to the administration office where he knew there was a spare set of exhibit keys. Of course, because Rich had lost his keys that meant he didn't have the key to get into the office either. So he tried to kick the door open. Rich ended up destroying the door. It wouldn't give, and with all the adrenalin pumping through his body he just splintered the whole door.

The next morning, Rich found his ring of keys caught in the tangle of juniper bushes where he had stood trying to fire the rifle. Then, what the heck? What's with this ladder leaning against the night house roof? It appeared to have been taken from the construction site next door. Then Rich returned to the night house and stepped through the keeper door into the outside tiger exhibit. Here he discovered two things that made the story a little clearer. One was that when this guy positioned the ladder and climbed onto the roof of the night house building, he apparently fashioned a knotted rope to ease down into the exhibit. He probably got the rope from the construction project too.

Then, a surprising find: There at the edge of the tiger's pond lay the guy's clothes all neatly folded up in a pile. The man was stark naked last night when he dragged himself in through the transfer door. Rich had assumed that he had been careless and somehow fallen into the exhibit, and that during the encounter the tiger ripped the clothes off him. It turns out Rich was pretty much wrong about everything.

We never found out for sure, but the rumor was that the man's leg was so shredded it had to be amputated above the knee. We heard that the guy had been at a party earlier that evening, drinking with his buddies. He apparently made some kind of bet concerning the tiger, and they dared him to go into the exhibit with him. (I'll leave the mystery of the clothing issue for you to solve.) We'll never know if the fool was at the zoo alone or if those drinking buddies had also been there, then abandoned him when the trouble started.

Given the details of the two stories, it's no surprise that alcohol was apparently involved in this and the rhino rodeo episode. Both of the young men's parents filed lawsuits against the zoo within days of these incidents. How ridiculous is that? But we employees never get to hear how any of the zoo's legal issues turn out. We always wondered, on what grounds could those lawsuits possibly be justified? With the influence of public intoxication and downright stupidity, wouldn't you think any sane judge should just toss those cases out of his court? Hopefully they were.

After the tiger incident, Rich always seemed to mysteriously disappear whenever a volunteer was needed to fill in for a fellow keeper.

JOSH HILTON, AGE 12

With a Gleam in His Eye

M any zoos unfortunately still exhibit some of their animals in settings with thick bars or heavy mesh and a concrete floor. It is financially prohibitive to upgrade each of them into the more desirable natural looking enclosures, so the tendency is to convert them gradually as funding allows.

At just the right moment one sunny afternoon, I happened to drive my golf cart past one of the zoo's ugly old exhibits made of chain link mesh. It housed a pair of endearing-looking but impish white-faced capuchin monkeys—the familiar "organ-grinder" monkeys of days gone by. They are pretty clever, and emote with an array of exaggerated facial expressions. A capuchin may be small—only about 16 inches long—but he's a tight bundle of surprisingly robust muscles. His handy, somewhat prehensile tail is nearly as long as his body.

I saw the capuchins' keeper, Kenny, standing just outside the enclosure, passing pieces of juicy chopped fruits and vegetables through the mesh to the monkeys. The male capuchin, "Hank," dominated the activity, selfishly grabbing every chunk of banana and juicy orange. He stuffed his cheeks as he kept his mate at bay. While bending down to sneak a grape to the little female anxiously waiting just below Hank, Kenny's head ended up just a little bit closer to the mesh. A little too close. That was all it took.

Hank became enraged when he realized that he was missing out on the delicious grape. In a flash he shoved his skinny arm through the chain link mesh and grabbed Kenny by his tousled blonde hair. The monkey gripped the keeper's curls with one hand while flashing a fearsome grimace that exposed ample canines. Then with a malicious gleam in his eye he pulled

DICK HILTON

Kenny close enough to seize a fistful of hair with his other hand. Although weighing only about 10 lbs., this feisty little animal had astonishing strength. His arms became powerful pistons, immediately turning Hank's head into a relentless pounding machine. While squatting on a branch, the nasty capuchin propped his feet against the cage for leverage and secured his sinuous tail around the branch. Then with all his might repeatedly slammed the keeper's head against the chain link mesh. WHAM! WHAM! WHAM! Over and over again.

I felt weak from empathy and sick to my stomach. It was all happening so fast, and so brutal to watch. I could tell Kenny's hair was being ripped out by the roots, causing excruciating pain. And the top of his head had been turned into a battering ram. Kenny was screaming and gripped with terror. He reflexively dropped the bucket of fruit, which banged boister-ously as it slammed against the concrete. But that wasn't enough to scare the monkey off; his emotions ran out of control. Kenny clenched his fingers, tightly gripping the mesh, trying in vain to brace his head against the blows. He screamed even louder, but the ecstatic capuchin still wouldn't let go. My yelling and arm waving as I raced toward the scene seemed only to incite the monkey further. That creepy grin grew even wider, as Hank re-peatedly raised his expressive eyebrows in spasms of flutter. The monkey's eyes darted back and forth continually—and with a particularly unnerving intensity—from Kenny's head, to my eyes, then back to Kenny's head, and so on. It was as if he couldn't contain himself, "Look at this! See what I've got? See what I'm doing?"

I headed for the hose so that maybe I could scare the monkey off with a spray of water, but in the meantime, Kenny, unable to stand any more of the ruthless head bashing, cleverly let go of the chain link with his right hand to feel for the rascal's feet that pressed against the mesh. Getting a good hard pinch on his big toe from Kenny, the startled monkey immediately released his hold on the keeper's hair and bounded away. And the horror ended, just that quickly! The entire incident took less than a minute but the memory will last a lifetime.

Zoo architects ideally try to design open-fronted, natural looking exhibits to provide the public an unobstructed view. But when misbehaving visitors slip behind fences or step over barriers installed for their safety designers are forced to create ever more imposing barriers. No amount of warning signs and guardrails seems to be enough for the handful of people intent on getting just a little bit closer for that "wild" interaction.

Not long after Kenny's run-in with the male capuchin, a father stupidly carried his little toddler around to the back of this same wretched exhibit, climbing over the guardrail "so she could get closer and feed the cute little monkeys." Fortunately, Hank only nipped the tip of one of her fingers, but it could have been disastrous. This and Kenny's unfortunate incident spurred the zoo into relocating the capuchins to an off-display holding cage until a safer situation could be devised.

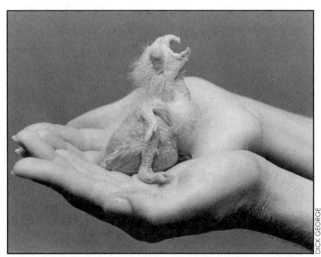

Most parrots raise their young in the dark hollow of a tree. It's a good thing since many look as frightful as this one...

...but in just a matter of weeks they transition to adorable.

Party Boat Pandemonium

The ultimate fate of that mischievous capuchin was that Hank, his mate, and two newly acquired young females were relocated to a spacious island in one of the zoo's lakes. Most primates don't know how to swim, so their inherent fear of water provides a natural escape deterrent. Lush palm and cottonwood trees and clumps of giant bamboo grew on the island, with branches dipping delicately at water's edge. We installed climbing ropes, snug sleeping boxes, and platforms for feeding and sunning. Delighted with the three girlfriends and new housing situation, Hank's behavior improved remarkably. Servicing the exhibit required a rowboat of course, which we also used to tend two other nearby islands that displayed spider monkeys and squirrel monkeys.

As part of the usual routine, early one morning Abby drove her golf cart along the lakeside road and pulled up to the dock. The keeper gathered up the trash bucket, rake, buckets of monkey chow and chopped produce, and bulky bag of fresh hay bedding from the bed of the cart. With her arms heavily loaded, she turned and plodded down the dock, headed for the boat. But, wait a minute; the boat's not here. What? Where could it be? She scanned the near shoreline and looked in the thick clumps of bamboo near the dock. Well, maybe the gardeners had borrowed the boat, she thought. Ooh, or worse, maybe she had somehow forgotten to moor it to the dock the day before. With a wave of dread beginning to sink in Abby set down all the stuff in her arms. This was too much like her first day of work a couple of years ago when she forgot to secure the boat on the island and all the spider monkeys went adrift. Abby's stomach began churning.

Then she happened to notice the chain they used to lock up the boat. It was there draped on the post all right, with the padlock still locked on it as if someone had taken the boat. But as she looked a little closer she could see that part of the chain was missing. Bolt cutters had obviously been used to neatly slice through one of the chain's links.

Abby jumped on her cart and began searching the shoreline all along the lake. On the farthest side she found the wayward boat suspiciously tangled in a thick mass of cattails. As she gingerly stepped into the shallow water to retrieve it that rotten egg smell of the sodden mud wafted up and made her gag. Holding her breath she took a few more steps and made a grab for the boat, dragging it back to shore. Great, Abby thought, now my shoes are going to always stink.

As she stomped her feet to get the excess water off she glanced over and, there in the boat lay three empty beer cans. And, what's this now? What are

Paddling to exhibit islands.

these reddish smears staining the oar handles? And what's all this on the bow and front seat of the boat? Big splatterings and puddles of what looked like dried blood added an ominous element of intrigue. Abby pulled the boat up on shore, and then sped off to the security and administration offices to make a report and see if anyone could shed light on this curious mystery. No one there knew anything about it either.

As she raced her cart back to the boat, Abby imagined horrible scenarios and worried about the welfare of the little monkeys. What grisly scene might she find out there on the island? Not wanting to get farther behind in the already delayed work routine (the zoo would be opening soon), she jumped into the boat. Trying to ignore the repulsive blood puddles she rowed over to the dock and tossed in all the stuff she'd left sitting there, then paddled headlong out to Capuchin Island. What a relief to find the animals looking and behaving normally. Then she noticed a few more pieces of the mysterious puzzle. Shredded remnants of cellophane potato chip bags, a six-pack of Bud, and a half empty beer can in the bushes made the following scenario most probable.

With obvious pre-meditation, and undoubted inebriation, an unknown number of people must have been intent on having a little malicious mischief at the zoo. They snuck in under the mantle of darkness armed with the bolt cutters, chips and beer. Thinking that continuing their drinking party on one of the islands would make them less likely to be detected by patrolling security guards, they made the unfortunate choice to take a little boating excursion to Capuchin Island. Either of the other two islands would have been a safer option but, as we have seen before, capuchins can be quite cantankerous. And primates often band together in a vicious show of aggression when they feel threatened. Surprised by the late night visit, Hank, the male capuchin monkey, and his little harem probably delighted in the opportunity to show off their daunting strength, agility, and fierce, long canines. No one but the perpetrators will ever know just how—and how much—blood was shed. We can only hope that the partiers at this gala affair may have also learned a much-needed temperance lesson.

This baby toco toucan takes his first wary look at the world before bravely fledging from the palm tree nest hollow the keepers made with a chain saw.

Didn't Get
What He Wanted,
But Got What He Deserved

Typically, a zoo displays small sedentary animals like reptiles and amphibians in a "reptile house" in a series of individual enclosures. The public views the animals through glass from the front of the enclosure while the keeper services them from the backside through a small, usually camouflaged, door. Often, the floorplan draws the viewers into a long tunnel-like passageway painted flat black so that the only source of light comes from inside the animals' quarters. The surrounding darkness enables the public to view the animals without the distraction of seeing their own reflection in the exhibit glass.

The reptile section of the zoo at the time of the following incident used a similar design, with a long row of some thirty reptile displays. One night a nefarious individual saw this shadowy area as a place to hide from the patrolling security guards. The event produced another mystery like the Capuchin Island escapade (see: "Party Boat Pandemonium"), this time with clues for the reptile keeper to piece together.

Entering his work area in the dim light of dawn, Jeff could scarcely make out a large dark spot on the concrete pathway that he figured must be sticky spilled soda from the day before. Anxious to start his chores with the snake collection he decided to tend to the mess later and thought no more of it. He headed for the reptile room and while walking around checking his animals, he couldn't be sure, but he thought he saw what looked like a lot of broken glass halfway down the long path of the dark viewing tunnel.

He hurried to the keeper service door, fumbled with his key to jam it into the lock, and flipped on the lights for all the exhibits. Then he sprinted back out and around to the tunnel, and ran down to where he found broken glass scattered all around in front of the exhibit of one of the more precious snakes. Grinning with relief, Jeff saw that the beautiful Sonoran mountain king snake with its glistening red, black, and white bands still laid peacefully coiled up in its display.

But then, ugh, what's all this? In the dim light his eyes focused on a tremendous amount of what appeared to be dark liquid—was it blood?—pooled amid the shards of glass on the ground. Splotches of blood also decorated the walls bordering the exhibit, and a bright red smear stained a big, jagged piece of glass still left in place in the window frame. Once he determined that none of the blood had come from the snake's body the keeper stopped holding his breath in apprehension. But, where did it come from?

Jeff hurried back through the keeper door of the reptile room and opened the service door of the king snake's display. He obviously couldn't leave the animal in there with the front open and broken glass all around. So he secured the snake into a lidded, large metal can that keepers used to temporarily transfer animals out of their displays. (This routine allowed the keepers to accomplish their chores without worrying about the animals' safety or their own.)

Then Jeff retraced the perpetrator's route. He followed faint, bloody footprints from the tunnel to the dark puddle he had noticed when he first arrived. Now that sunlight flooded the sidewalk he could clearly see that it was a good deal of congealed blood staining the concrete. He continued on the ensanguined trail that took him through tangles of thorny pyracantha bushes to the zoo's 8-foot-high perimeter fence, topped with three rows of barbed wire. There, at the foot of the fence, lay a soggy, blood-saturated pillowcase, which the desperado had apparently brought along to slip his booty into. Instead he'd had to use it to stanch the pulsing flow of vital fluid from his arm's severed artery. We never did learn the culprit's identity, but hopefully this would-be thief learned as enduring a lesson as the beer drinkers of Capuchin Island.

The Seaweed Monster

"W as it you, Rich, that ran a golf cart into the zoo lake?" asked Ben at lunch one day.

"Yeah, it was me, but it was the Datsun pickup truck, not the cart," Rich replied. "The white truck, the one Kenny shot a hole in."

"What do you mean that Kenny shot a hole in?"

"Kenny set a palm tree on fire," Rich said, "to smoke out this big wild raccoon that had been killing ducks at the lakeshore each night. He hadn't been able to live trap it. Kenny went to grab the rifle to shoot the raccoon and accidentally shot the truck instead! I remember reading the keepers' Daily Reports at the end of that day, and on Kenny's under 'Observations' it said: 'Burned down two palm trees in crane exhibit.' Under 'Maintenance Request' was: 'Repair Datsun door—shot hole through door.' I couldn't believe what I'd just read! He just casually reported that he burned down two palm trees and shot the truck! He never did get the raccoon, but I guess it moved on to the marsh in the park outside the zoo after all that commotion because we didn't lose any more ducks.

"Anyway, I was starting my evening rounds and parked the truck at the lake between the snack bar and the old capuchin monkey exhibit. Then I walked over to the jaguar night house. A snack bar kid—I can't remember which one it was now—was goofing around and thought it'd be funny to hide the truck on me. He put it in neutral, then released the brake and rolled it, but it got away from him. It picked up speed and rolled right down into the lake, ending up in the water all the way up to the roof!

"The next day I had to swim into the lake and attach a tow chain around the chassis of the truck. It took forever because the water was so murky I couldn't see what I was doing; I had to do everything by feel. And man was that water cold. My hands got so cold my fingers wouldn't work.

After I finally got the chain attached I crawled in the cab to steer and work the brakes as they hauled the truck out. When we got to the shore I opened the door and all that water that filled the cab came gushing out, and my lap was like a big strainer. My pants were just covered with green, thick, gloppy algae. Luckily the snack bar kid confessed that he'd started it rolling as a practical joke, otherwise I would've thought I'd left it out of gear and taken the rap for it."

Ben asked if the truck was salvageable. "Yeah," Rich chuckled, "but it sat in dry dock for a long time and needed a lot of work. It was really funny because it was mid-summer when you get that real bad algae growth around the edges of the lake. The truck looked like some kind of seaweed monster when they pulled it out. I mean there were weeds and algae hanging from everywhere. Not just from the bottom and sides of the truck, but from the seats, the dash, the rear view mirror and steering wheel, too. It was just covered with the weeds and all slimy and green. And you know that really distinctive smell algae has? It just permeated it. And in the heat, it stunk all summer long. I just couldn't believe it that night when I came out of the jaguar night house and saw my truck slowly sinking into the lake!"

Disarmingly Beautiful Waterfowl

Most people know how notoriously aggressive geese are when protecting their nests or young. The Nene (pronounced "nay-nay") goose of Hawaii is a demure, more sweet-tempered version of the Canada goose, but still quite defensive during breeding season. One day I leaned down to check on the four creamy-white eggs in the nest of our pair of Nene. It was about time for them to be hatching. I gently nudged my hand under the female's breast as she stubbornly sat warming the large eggs. She stared straight ahead, motionless. It was as if she thought, If I ignore her this can't really be happening.

Her angry protective mate burst out from under some nearby bushes and stopped short, assessing the situation with intense stares. He rose up in an extreme vertical posture, then stretched his neck out into an oddly hunched position perpendicular to his body. He honked and hissed at me with his beak wide open and narrow pink tongue sticking out. Powered by snappy wingbeats, he ran over to us on the tippy-toes of his webbed feet. I cringed as he began to bite at my long, dangling hair while fumbling to replace the egg still in my hand. I don't know which of us was more astounded when I straightened up as this outraged goose, wildly flapping his wings, swung back and forth by his beak from my hair. The two of us together moved in the rhythm of a pendulum. He refused to release his tenacious

Hawaii's endangered nene goose.

DICK GEORGE

grip until I bent down to gently set his feet back on the ground.

But this was nothing compared to the behavior of the handsome black swan of Australia with its frilly black plumage and scarlet beak....

My arms loaded with buckets of monkey chow, chopped produce, and a bag of fresh bedding, I waded through the knee-deep water the 20 feet or so to Squirrel Monkey Island to care for the impatient little group of monkeys. I wore bulky hip waders sized for a man with big feet. The boot part extended a good four inches longer than my toes. If I could move fast enough I bet I could have water-skied in them.

I also carried a long-handled deck broom locked in the crook of my elbow, but there was no pond on the island to scrub. The broom served as my defense against "Ozzie," our fierce Australian black swan. This was breeding season, and he steadfastly guarded his mate and nest full of five big white eggs on the backside of a neighboring island. Anyone violating his territory—demarked by a line that only he could discern—became fair game for his ire. The plan was that the length of the broom handle would keep the cob (male swan) from getting too close to me while the soft brush bristles wouldn't hurt him if he attacked.

Finished with my chores on the island, I scanned the vicinity for the swan. Good, no sign of him. He must be napping next to the nest. I cautiously plopped my foot with the big boot onto the slippery algae-encrusted rocks under the water. I glanced up and, oh no. Where did he come from?

Ozzie looked like a torpedo skimming the water. Within seconds, mighty paddle strokes powered by his huge webbed feet brought the cob within striking distance. He ruffled out his neck feathers, doubling the appearance of his neck size. His stern body posture and raised wings completed the image, succeeding in his intimidation strategy. Ozzie glared at me with his freaky red eyes while aggressively flailing at my broom with brisk wing beats. To my horror, after the third whack he knocked the scrub brush off and sent it splashing into the water. I stood there, dumbfounded, with only the buckets and the long wooden handle of the broom in my hands.

Now defenseless, I made a hasty retreat back to the sanctuary of the island. Not wanting him to follow after me on land I edged along the shore of the island, enticing him to keep paddling after me. Haphazard jumbles of big, rounded river rocks ringed the small island. This made the circumference much longer and more difficult for Ozzie to maneuver through than my trek around the grassy

Australian black swan, aka "The Torpedo."

shore perimeter, even in the cumbersome boots. I made him paddle at a fast pace for several speedy circumnavigations of the island, tiring him enough so I could be confident of the possibility of my escaping unscathed. Meanwhile, the confused troop of squirrel monkeys retreated to the tops of the trees to get as far from this unusual circus as possible.

Once I had the exhausted cob positioned on the far backside, I clomped straight across the island to my departure point. Splashing wildly in the awkward boots, I plunged onto the submerged rocks and then heaved the buckets across to the far shore. I threw my arms out to try to keep my balance and sloshed through the deepening water as hastily as I could manage. Oh, now what? His legs may have been worn out from all that paddling, but now the swan was using his *wings* to propel his body across the water! How could he have covered that much distance so fast? Just three more short steps separated me from making it safely out of the water when Ozzie caught up and fiercely trounced my legs with the leading edge of his wings. (That humerus bone is a hefty one in a bird as big as a swan and leaves a good bruise.) As a final insult, he encouraged my cowardly retreat with a really rude goosing before I managed to escape up the steep shore. Obviously bragging, a proud Ozzie cruised back and forth in the water, vocalizing to his mate about his glorious victory.

The next day when I arrived to service the island the long-handled deck broom again rested in the crook of my arm, but this time with a big long screw securely affixing the brush to the handle.

One day the male swan became so overly zealous protecting his cygnets he chased a zoo gardener across the bridge, ending up in a different lake from his nest.

Would've Made a Good Picture

A pachyderm handler receives a lot of intense, specialized training and tends to stay in that job for the long-term. Meanwhile the elephants need a protracted period of adjustment to the person. They learn to trust their keeper and be willing to respond to commands. I rarely worked with elephants during my career because I never trained to be a handler. I would only pitch in when the keepers needed an extra hand, raking the outside yard while the two young female African elephants stayed safely locked inside their night house or in the side yard. Here the spacing of a row of massive pillars allows a keeper to easily pass through, but restricts an elephant. The day of the following particular incident I was very new on the job, and quite unwise.

One hot summer afternoon, massive sooty clouds jostled for position while deep muffled thunder rumbled in the distance. We needed the rain, but the storm was mostly a tease. It was probably raining in torrents in the mountains miles away, but wasn't amounting to much here in the city. As I drove past the elephant exhibit in the light drizzle I noticed something odd in my peripheral vision. I stopped my cart and hopped off to take a look. It appeared that a zoo visitor must've accidentally dropped a film canister next to the guardrail, where it rolled within reach of the elephants. With their dexterous trunks they had managed to pull the film out of the canister and were eagerly inspecting it. Drat, wouldn't you know. Not finding any elephant keepers nearby, I felt intervention was crucial before they ingested nasty chemicals by mouthing or, worse yet, eating the strip of celluloid.

The ground, hard-packed from years of elephant traffic, wouldn't let the rain soak in and so the water slowly sprawled across in rivulets and puddles. The dampened dirt stuck in clumps to the bottom of my shoes as I tentatively entered the exhibit. I hoped their youth and unfamiliarity with me would make them retreat to a far part of their 5-acre yard. I hadn't gone more than a few steps, still about 20 yards from "Kintaya," when she became aware of my presence. Not hesitating for a moment, she barreled toward me with her trunk extended up and those big ears sticking out and flapping—the classic charge. With each footstep she deliberately skidded hard into the soggy dirt, trying to kick up clouds of dust to add to the grand illusion of power and size. And her immature voice tried its best—quite effectively—to warn me that her "bluff" meant serious business. I froze, nearly catatonic with fear. For an elephant only about half-grown, Kintaya sure seemed to be a whole lot larger all of a sudden. I spun around and bolted back to the gate, desperate to slip between the big pillars before she caught up with me.

It turned out that my intrusion proved successful after all. Both elephants forgot about the film while their sensitive nostrils investigated these different-smelling footprints in the mud. This distraction gave me time to contact their keepers (as I should have done in the first place), who arrived expeditiously to retrieve the film.

Some time later, this same elephant who had given me chase didn't seem to like a new keeper in training. Perhaps Kintaya was leery because John was the first male handler she had ever interacted with.

Unobserved by the two keepers busily raking the elephant yard one morning, step by slow deliberate step Kintaya sidled up close to them. Then, without any warning, she reached out her trunk and, using it like a grappling hook, snagged John by the ankle and flipped him right over the wheelbarrow. With the breath knocked out of him, John landed hard on the ground with the wheelbarrow between himself and the elephant. If her intent had been serious aggression she might have continued her attack with more tragic results. It may have just been Kintaya's way of testing him, or letting him know that she wasn't too accepting of him yet. But for John, the message was dire enough that he decided never to work with elephants again.

~~~~~~

These were serious incidents not to be taken lightly. Extremely intelligent and prone to boredom, elephants need distractions and lots of them. They weigh 4 to 5 tons and tower over their handlers at a height of up to 9 feet, so elephants really don't have to do anything they decide not to. Instead, they seem to respond because they enjoy the relationship with the keepers, and the stimulation of the interactions. Aggressive pachyderms, especially testosterone-driven males in "musth" (breeding condition), can cause serious injuries and occasionally the death of a handler. They have been known to knock a keeper over and step on him or kneel down, mashing into him with their great forehead—breaking his back. Or they might simply lean, squashing the keeper between elephant and wall with their massive bulk.

Over the years, handlers' interactions with their elephants have become more intimate and varied, creating a strong bond. Besides training and bathing, elephants tolerate toenail trimming, blood drawing and other medical treatments, and even artificial insemination. This increased contact puts keepers and zoo veterinarians at much higher risk for potential injury. So along with these more intense interactions, safer interfacing methods have been devised known as "protective contact." Whenever possible, keepers perform their chores with the elephants on the other side of some form of barrier, such as a door so massive it must operate with hydraulics, or pillars spaced wide enough for a keeper and an elephant's leg to fit through but too narrow for her body. For a pedicure, for instance, on command an elephant sticks her leg through two pillars and places her foot onto a stool that sits on the keeper's side of the barrier. Then the essential nail trimming and filing can be performed with little risk to the keepers. In the wild, elephants' toenails naturally wear down as they roam great distances. The nails of more sedentary zoo elephants can painfully split into the quick if keepers don't keep them filed back.

For many zoo animals, "behavioral enrichments" center on feeding to draw out that activity. For example, on a hot summer day the elephants may bathe in their exhibit's large pond. For added amusement, keepers fill a 2-foot-diameter rubber tub with water and add things like chopped apples, celery, and carrots. They freeze the whole thing solid, and then toss the ice block into the elephant's pond. The pachyderms enjoy the challenge of smashing the floating block, gradually gaining access to the colorful prizes as the big ice chunks slowly melt.

An adult elephant consumes 125 lbs. of hay, herbivore pellets, fruits and vegetables daily. The food just dropped off in big piles twice a day bores them. It is certainly more labor intensive for keepers, but the animals prefer feedings broken into numerous intervals throughout the day and searching for foods hidden in surprising locations. This is true not just for elephants but also for many different zoo animals, especially primates and bears. Coming up with enrichment ideas challenges a keeper's creativity. Our efforts are rewarded with the animals' enthusiastic responses to the clever inspirations. It can be entertaining for zoo visitors to observe as well, so everyone wins.

KRISTIN HILTON

Just a Little Love Nip

S ome keepers jeopardize their own health by working at this chosen profession. Jennifer is short and energetic with long, wavy black hair. She suffers from severe asthma, and seems to be allergic to everything. Jennifer constantly blows her nose and wheezes while rubbing itchy red eyes, but can't imagine having any other job. One of her favorite zoo animals is the big male lowland gorilla, "Moboko." Starting at about age twelve, a male gorilla develops a distinctive patch of gray hair between the shoulder blades, which increases with maturity to cover his entire back, butt, and thighs (hence the term "silverback"). At the beginning of the following incident our handsome guy was in his prime, his mantle of silver hair glittering in the sunlight.

For some reason, Moboko began to lose interest in eating. Always pretty mellow and sedentary, this 30-year-old great ape became increasingly lethargic. Weight loss became dramatic and his face gaunt and drawn. He also developed a persistent and harsh, phlegmy cough. The vet decided this wasn't something transitory—we needed to sedate the gorilla for a complete physical and battery of tests.

The lab results verified a diagnosis of valley fever (coccidioidomycosis), a sometimes-serious infection caused by the inhalation of fungus spores found in dusty desert soil. It is prevalent in certain areas of the arid American southwest. In most cases, an infected human may exhibit no symptoms at all, while others may think they have had a cold. Some can show no symptoms whatsoever until 20 years later. In a rare form of the disease, which often carries a high death rate, the infection spreads from the lungs to the bones, liver, brain, and heart. Individuals with compromised immune systems suffer particular vulnerability to the more serious infections. Valley fever affects dogs as well as humans, and as we tragically discovered over the years, other primates, kangaroos and even warthogs.

Besides strong daily medication, Moboko needed constant encouragement to eat to keep up his strength. He continued to suffer a lack of appetite, gradually appearing withered with such drastic weight loss. His chestnut brown eyes looked glassy and crusted in the corners. And his once lustrous black and silver coat became matted in places and had no sheen. Surely poor Moboko was slowly dying.

Alarmed at his rapidly deteriorating condition, all the keepers made special efforts to entice Moboko to eat more. One day Jennifer came to visit with some tasty carrot cake with walnuts and raisins that she baked especially for him. The emaciated gorilla perked up a bit when he saw her, but still lolled about in his bed of hay. After lots of sweet-talking and tempting, he finally got curious enough to come see what she had so thoughtfully brought.

As she broke the carrot cake into bite-size morsels Jennifer knew she shouldn't be standing so near his reach, but foolishly assumed that he was too ill to be a danger. With astonishing speed Moboko injected his hand between the bars and grabbed her wrist. He pulled her arm to his lips, bit her forearm, and then just as quickly released her hand. It all happened so fast Jennifer had no chance to react. She stepped back and, stunned speechless, envisioned how she could have been pulled through the bars, piece by piece. Moboko had never been aggressive with anyone before and indeed, this seemed more like a "love nip" than an attack.

This little bite barely even drew any blood, and for most people probably wouldn't be a problem. But with all of poor Jennifer's allergies, the gorilla's oral bacteria entering the wound made her extremely ill. In no time at all, the infection spread to the bone below the wound. It took several rounds of various antibiotics to find one that Jennifer wasn't allergic to and that her body finally responded to. If the medications had failed, she faced amputation as the only way to stop this serious infection.

Even after enduring so much trauma, Jennifer never stopped indulging the gorilla. She just made a point to never be anywhere near his range of grasp. It took a long time, but with good veterinary care and determined spoiling from keepers Moboko eventually rallied to once again become the robust and majestic 500-lb. silverback he had once been.

As big and impressive as the two gorillas were, for some reason Moboko and his mate "Sokwe" seemed utterly terrified of nuns. This was back when sisters wore the traditional long, flowing black habit with white and black headdress. If they spotted nuns approaching, the gorillas would scramble to retreat to the only corner of their exhibit where they could be pretty much out of sight from the public. Occasionally peeking from their hiding spots, Moboko and Sokwe stayed hidden until the nuns gave up and moved on. Only then would the gorillas venture back out.

Abundant palm fronds on the zoo grounds provide many diverse uses such as: something for animals to play with or lie down on; to chew up or otherwise destroy; visual barrier, shade material, shelter or roofing; and even torn into fibers for birds' nest material.

One time the gorilla keeper finally got to witness this rare and unusual behavior he had only heard about. On that day, the two gorillas spotted three nuns with a bunch of students from a parochial school approaching and tripped over each other as they ran to hide. The women were very patient but, after a time, they gave up waiting for the apes to reappear and strolled off to the next exhibit. With his brown eyes flashing, Moboko charged out of his hiding place and raced across the exhibit toward where the nuns had just been standing. He stopped short, then stood up defiant and tall and dramatically beat his bare chest, cupping his big hands to augment the sound. The proud ape leaned forward in a daunting Schwarzenegger-esque pose. He added a menacing stare at the backs of the "retreating" nuns to emphasize the point that he had managed to chase them off. Meanwhile the students and other zoo visitors dashed back forming a big crowd and loudly exclaimed their awe at Moboko's impressive show. All that commotion caught the distant nuns' attention, so they rushed back only to be frustrated yet again to see an empty exhibit when Moboko and Sokwe disappeared, retreating to their hiding spot.

Late one summer afternoon Rich and Kyle were returning the female gorilla from a visit to a nearby medical center. Along the route, they delighted in seeing the shocked expressions on the faces of drivers and pedestrians as they noticed this most unusual passenger. By the time they returned to the zoo grounds it was just getting to be dusk and the zoo was closed. Aside from a security guard at the entrance the keepers and gorilla were alone.

Kyle suddenly had an idea and hopped out of the van. He slid open the panel door and secured it in place. For the next half hour, the gorilla sat inside the van in her mesh transfer crate transfixed on the scenery as the keepers leisurely drove throughout the zoo, taking a long route back to her exhibit. Kyle paused at the larger exhibits to give her a chance to absorb the view, and she seemed especially enamored of the elephants. At the end of the tour Kyle stopped the vehicle in front of the gorilla exhibit for a long while to let Sokwe see her own living area from this new perspective.

Rich and Kyle took a risk of getting in trouble if the curator found out about this little adventure, but were so elated to be able to share the experience with Sokwe that they felt it was worth any reprimand.

Impressionable Pachyderm

One thing that elephants seem to be quite good at is standing around in one place. For safety, our small mixed group of Asian and African elephants spends the night in indoor quarters, but during the day they freely roam their spacious 5-acre exhibit. For bathing, a huge concrete pond sits in the vicinity of the night house. A gradually sloping, shallow perimeter leads to the middle of the water that's deep enough for the bathing beauties to completely submerge themselves. As much roaming as elephants do in the wild, you would think that they would take advantage of all that acreage to explore. Yet the only time they venture anywhere but the half-acre or so between the pond and their night house is when the keepers force them to by distributing food out in the far reaches. Lush grass carpets the exhibit except for the dustbowl of that hangout area where the soil is so compacted nothing can grow.

One day "Cleo" seemed bored, just wistfully waiting for the keepers' raking to end so she could get some attention. She leaned against the wall, mindlessly swinging her foot about in a patch of loose dirt. From a distance it looked to one of the keepers like this Asiatic elephant was actually doodling. From the humble beginnings of Cleo rubbing her foot around, the keepers were inspired to supply her with large sheets of paper on the ground and an oversized pencil she could clench with her trunk. This gradually progressed to a much more complex and stimulating activity for the elephant that she couldn't enjoy more. She became so proficient at painting creations on artist canvases that she exhibited her own show at a posh local art gallery. The zoo's public relations director even published a cute children's book about her unique talent.

As part of the behavioral enrichment program, once a week or so the keepers set up an easel with a canvas. They hold out four or five variously sized artist brushes and Cleo gently touches her choice with her trunk. She then selects a color of non-toxic paint, the keeper loads it onto the brush, and Cleo grasps it with the agile tip of her trunk. The creative elephant is then free to let her talented trunk produce whatever art composition naturally comes about.

DICK GEORGE

By the way, did you know that there are an astounding *40,000* different muscles in an elephant's versatile trunk? Compare that to just 650 muscles in the entire human body. An evolutionary marvel, the tapered proboscis combines both the nose and upper lip, transforming them into a single, amazingly utilitarian appendage. A "finger" projects at the end tip of the trunk; the African elephant has one on the top and one on the bottom, while the Asiatic has a single one on the top.

Have you ever considered just how many things an elephant can do with its trunk? Obviously used for breathing and smelling as with any other nose, it also makes a nice resonance chamber for enhancing vocalizations. The trunk is handy for sucking up water (about 16 inches up the nostrils), then squirting it into the mouth for a drink or over the body for a bath. Each trunkful may hold between 1 and 2 gallons of water. Wrapping the end of the trunk around a scoopful of dusty dirt and tossing it over the back helps prevent sunburn and deters annoying insects. It's agile enough to strip leaves off a branch, sensitive enough to pick up a small pebble, yet strong enough to uproot a tree. Forcefully blowing air out the nostrils while mucking about under water, elephants disperse silt to expose nutritionally crucial minerals. It can be a handy assist for a youngster trying to exit a slippery pond edge. Using the trunk as an extension pole, an elephant can reach far up into trees to obtain food, then place it directly in his mouth. Scratching an itch is easy, and what a weapon it can be against predators. It's a handy snorkel when swimming, and great for greeting and caressing fellow pachyderms—or for aggressive interactions. And, of course, everyone is familiar with an agitated elephant's imposing appearance when they raise the trunk, flap their ears, and stridently bugle during a threat display. Don't you wish you had a handy trunk? I sure do—it would be even better than a monkey's prehensile tail!

But, back to Cleo's painting. When she's inspired to change to a different color or brush size the selection process begins again. This continues until, ebullient, she raises and wiggles her trunk, signifying that she's decided that the creation is done. The keepers then hand Cleo an uncapped marking pen to "sign" her painting. She steps back and with talented trunk raised high, shakes her head, flaps her ears, and then takes a bow while squeaking and trumpeting exuberantly. She's a real ham.

This might be just another story about a zoo animal that paints, which perhaps isn't so unique nowadays, except that in Cleo's case interesting inspirations may possibly be linked to her paintings. One day when a zoo visitor needed paramedics, the red fire truck sped right past the elephant yard with siren wailing. The next time Cleo painted the only colors she chose were red and a touch of black, which was unusual as she tended to make wildly colorful compositions. Another day, a tow-headed little girl wearing a pastel pink and blue sweater walked with a group of VIPs visiting the elephants in their night house. The next time she painted, Cleo chose only pastel pink, yellow, and blue for the color scheme. What do you think, coincidences?

It's odd how sometimes your job can affect your personal life in an unexpected way. Such was the case for Kelly, one of the elephant keepers. She stopped by the grocery store for a few items on her way home from work one day. She often did. Nothing unusual about that. Except that this time, the cashier suddenly looked up at Kelly with a confounded look on her face. "It's you!" she exclaimed as she wrinkled up her nose in disgust. "You're what stinks!"

Kelly knew that elephant manure, especially when roasted by the summer sun, had a unique stench that could permeate her clothes and hair and make them rather fragrant. After all these years though, she never even really thought about it anymore. Throughout the day her nose got used to the smell and she didn't realize just how much the powerful odor still clung to her. After this embarrassing incident with the cashier she got to thinking, and as she reflected back to previous visits to the crowded market she made an appalling realization. Often times she had noticed that she suddenly became the only person standing in the checkout line. It wasn't that the other shoppers had suddenly remembered another necessity to seek out, or politeness in letting Kelly go ahead of them. Now she knew the real reason....

Need a Light?

Sometimes, being too trusting of dangerous animals can get a keeper into serious trouble. One day Joe was in the chimpanzee night quarters playing with "Zippy," reaching through the bars and roughhousing with him—an absolute no-no and he certainly knew it. Chimps may stand up to 5 feet tall and weigh only about 100 lbs., but that sinewy build is all muscle. By contrast, Joe was a big bruiser at 6'4" and 250 lbs. He had worked with Zippy for many years and became too familiar and complacent with him. And he knew that the sly chimp often took an opportunity to prove how macho he could be.

Maybe Zip wasn't in the mood to play, or wanted to show who he thought held dominance. For whatever reason, as the keeper playfully tousled the chimp's hair, Zippy turned on him and bit into Joe's hand. His sharp canines deeply gouged Joe's tender flesh into parallel bloody tracks the entire distance of the keeper's palm from wrist to pinky finger. It took about sixty stitches and several weeks on intravenous antibiotics to heal the ragged wounds. Joe was as fortunate as Jennifer (who'd had the "love nip" from the gorilla) to find a treatment that worked.

Keeping this history on unpredictable Zippy in mind, any time I interacted with him I carefully avoided giving him opportunities to grab me through the bars of his night house. This could be inconvenient and difficult at times. Grooming is an important part of socialization and comfort for chimps. Zippy loved all the attention, especially because he inhabited the exhibit by himself. (We tried roommates a couple of times before with results that left no doubt—Zip was too imprinted on humans to coexist with one of his own kind.) He would often solicit a soothing session of back scratching by leaning against the bars while softly hooting.

Cute and charismatic, Zip was exceptionally personable, and he had an intense interest in women. It was hard to believe that there could ever be an aggressive incident with him. But the risk of being pulled into the range of his brawny arms and imposing teeth mandated constant caution. We trained him to stretch up and grasp the bars above his head to give the keeper a bit of an extra safety measure during close encounter situations like a pedicure or giving him a drink of juice. This behavior conditioning was especially helpful when we needed to administer medication.

Zippy, raised by humans before coming to the zoo, often surprised us with some unique behaviors. For instance, he knew the function of a washcloth, enthusiastically rubbing a dampened one over his head and face. He liked to run a brush through the sparse hair on his arms and legs. His valiant attempts to use a toothbrush would impress a dentist. He also let me trim the thick nails on his fingers and toes, but only if I sort of reciprocated, as in the following.

He had a bit of a foot fetish. Zippy loved to admire and smell shoes and feet. He'd point to my foot and impatiently vocalize while hopping up and down. If I took my shoe off for him, he was instantly transfixed and spent a good deal of time sniffing it as I held it near the bars. Once finished with the shoe he would excitedly point to my sock. After I took that off and let him scrutinize my foot, Zip then wanted to sniff my toes. Of course, that was allowed only out of reaching distance. (Just how strong did my feet smell?!) He often expressed curiosity about what might be up my pant leg or under my shirt, only I declined to satisfy that nosiness...but I could understand his kinky fascinations when considering his pre-zoo lifestyle.

Some of Zippy's early history included rather bizarre and demeaning activities, involving of all things, boxing matches with other chimps and nightclub work. In the 1950s when Zip was just a youngster, his owner would dress him in a little maroon tuxedo and drive him around town. He learned to smoke cigarettes and cigars. (Years later, if a smoker stood outside his zoo exhibit, Zippy would point eagerly to the cigarette trying to solicit a puff.) The owner took him to nightclubs, where the chimp would light patrons' cigarettes with a lighter. To everyone's amusement he'd put on a big show while coyly peeking up ladies' dresses. The story goes that, after doing the night club circuits for some time, his exceptional career came to an abrupt end when he broke a couple of ribs of a woman that he hugged just a little too enthusiastically.

In his later years at the zoo, keepers introduced Zippy to the activity of applying non-toxic paints to canvas. Many zoos employ this behavioral enrichment for their great apes and pachyderms to prevent boredom. Zoos sometimes sell the paintings as fundraisers or give them as special gifts. At about age 60 Zippy took to the finger painting like he'd been waiting his whole life to delve into it. He then progressed to using brushes, producing inspirational creations with a sensitive balance of design and color. Maybe we should rename him Grandpa Moses…?

KRISTIN HILTON

The brown pelican chick that changed my life. She diverted my career from an interest in felines to a devotion to birds. How can you not become endeared to this prehistoric-looking creature?

Zippy's New Toy

Gary, a seasoned, older animal keeper, never had any formal training but was a "natural" working with animals. Some keepers have awesome talent that way—they just have an innate knack for reading animal behavior and Gary certainly ran in that pack. He could also express a somewhat acerbic sense of humor, and nobody enjoyed being the butt of his practical jokes.

After some 25 years at the same job, he didn't need a boss. Gary, quite rigid in his ways, had his work routine as efficient as it could ever be. Not a moment was wasted. This stubborn man resisted any suggested changes, finding ways to make them fail. The zoo had just created a new head keeper position. He resented the notion of having someone supervise him, and who could blame him. And what could make it even worse for Gary? This new boss was a woman. And worse for me—*I* was that new head keeper.

I briefly met most of the staff then spent the rest of my first day in meetings and setting up my office. The morning of my second day on this new job, disaster struck. Gary burst into the office, waving his arms in a frenzy and yelling, "You'd better do something quick. The elephant has gotten out and he's on a rampage! The zoo just opened and lots of people are already on the grounds!" Then he spun around and ran back out the door.

Adrenalin stoked my first reactions, and I quickly considered various emergency procedure options. This zoo was new to me and so I had more questions than answers. How will we get people safely out? Should I call the vet or the curator first? How manageable is this escaped animal…until I abruptly remembered that this particular zoo didn't *have* any elephants. In the distance, I could see Gary chuckling as he headed back to work. Feelings of despair replaced the adrenalin surge, and I found myself questioning my career move to this zoo.

This somewhat arrogant keeper ultimately had to eat some humble pie though, when he inadvertently caused a grave situation at the chimpanzee exhibit. Each morning, with the chimp locked inside his night quarters, the keeper entered the outside display through a service door. He lugged in an aluminum ladder in order to hose the upper level of rockwork. After Gary finished cleaning the exhibit one day, as per usual he returned to the night house and shifted the big male chimp, Zippy, through the short transfer door from the night quarters outside to the display. Within seconds, Gary heard all kinds of loud banging noises going on out there. With a tight knot forming in his stomach, he raced out of the night house around to the front of the exhibit to see what the commotion was. He groaned with dismay when he saw that he had somehow forgotten to pull the ladder out before moving Zippy outside.

Oh, what a magnificent large and shiny novelty! Zip hooted with delight over his new "enrichment device," dragging the ladder around with a great clanging racket. He just loved really noisy things. Gary's various attempts to entice Zip back into the night house failed of course. How ridiculous to even think that he might leave such a wondrous thing. After about ten minutes of bashing and pitching the ladder about, the exuberant chimp decided that he'd like to take it into his night quarters. Except that only a chimp could pass through the transfer door, certainly not an 8-foot-long ladder and at a sharp angle around a corner! But he was determined to get it in there and just kept pushing. Now the ladder jammed the doorway completely, so Zippy couldn't be locked inside the night quarters even if he could be coaxed to come in. This made it utterly impossible for Gary to retrieve the ladder.

The zoo had only just opened, so luckily only four visitors roamed about. With apologies and a brief explanation, we quickly ushered them out and closed the zoo so we could focus all our attention on solving this dilemma. Gary and the rest of the staff assembled in the office, phoning the veterinarian to calculate a possible tranquilizer dosage and brainstorming other alternatives. Meanwhile, I wandered over to the exhibit.

After a few minutes of forceful but futile shoving, Zippy contorted his body so he could slide past the jammed ladder back into his night house. Now, with incessant tugging, he was intent on coercing the ladder through the doorway from the other direction. With each pull he got visibly frustrated with its lack of cooperation. With a few calls of his name it was easy for me to lure the exasperated chimp into squeezing back outside because he really liked women. And now he had this great new plaything to show off. His eyes were intense and gleaming, and I had never seen Zip this excited. He didn't know what to do with himself. He hooted in wild crescendos while grinning to expose his Draculean canines. He exaggerated the arch of his back to look taller. And every sparse hair on his wiry body stuck out from big goose bumps

CINDY BARRY

as he swaggered around with his elbows forward and shoulders raised up—all of which had the effect of emphasizing Zippy's masculinity. He began rattling and yanking on the ladder to impress me with his vigor. When it suddenly popped free of the doorway, he hefted it over his head like a prize-winning weightlifter. Then with an incredible surge of strength, the chimp flung the ladder five feet up the rockwork toward the upper level. The clattering cacophony of it cascading back down, and heading right toward him, terrified the ape, so I ran around back into the night house while yelling his name. He wasted no time in dashing through his now ladder-free doorway to be inside with me, leaving his loud new toy behind. I promptly slammed the transfer door shut in his wake. End of problem.

I don't think Gary ever quite forgave me for solving the predicament so easily, but I never had to worry about being the butt of his sadistic jokes again.

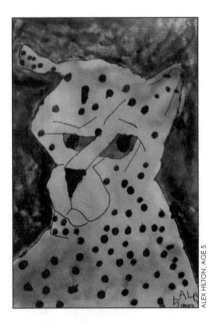

ALEX HILTON, AGE 5

Naughty Nose

With his athletic build and sleek dark hair, Jon typified a fit and enthusiastic keeper. He was just starting the evening keeper duties late one particularly rainy Saturday afternoon, and the curator and one security guard were the only other people on the grounds. Most of the exhibits at this zoo were outdoors, and with the torrential rain not one visitor had ventured to the zoo since it opened. The unusually lousy weather forced all the concessions to close. The keepers, waterlogged and cold, had been allowed to go home early once completing their minimum chores.

Jon winced as he slid out of the truck and glanced up at the monstrous thunderclouds trudging across the inky sky. They had already hemorrhaged a record amount of precipitation. It didn't seem possible that they could wring out any more moisture, but the raindrops pelted even harder in the gusts of wind. Usually he enjoyed the pungent odor of wet creosote bushes, but not so much today.

Because of the soaking weather, to save time Jon made a poor decision. This afternoon was the only time that he deliberately failed to put the lock through the latch to the gate of the Grevy's zebras' off-exhibit yard. He entered the night house and then let the female zebra in from her exhibit. She seemed anxious to get in out of the rain and trotted through the passageway into the barn. But then she continued right on through to the outside yard, heading straight to that gate. It was if she knew. Jon gasped when he recalled that he hadn't slipped the lock through the latch, but thought to himself, It's no big deal. The latch is down on the gatepost. And besides, she's not going to want to stay outside in this awful weather and she'll come right back into the night house.

When Jon first began to work in the African animals' exhibits, his trainers emphasized that you shouldn't just flip the latch shut on the zebras' chain link gate—always stick a lock through it. A zebra is smart enough to flip the latch up with its nose, push open the gate, and then take off.

Grevy's zebra

Just as all those dire warnings came back to him he froze in horror when, sure enough, she flipped the latch with her nose, nudged open the gate, and off she went! Right at that moment, the dark sky split with dramatic, strobe light cracks of lightning. The thickness of the moisture in the air muffled the rolling booms of thunder that rumbled along after. The spooked zebra galloped over the rise toward the gorilla exhibit where bales of hay sat stacked in an open-sided shed. Quickly forgetting the scary noises, she nonchalantly veered over to the pile and grabbed a mouthful of hay, then ran past the shed, heading up the hill toward the bighorn sheep exhibit.

Dreadful thoughts ran through Jon's head. He recalled that zebras have a deadly kick, they weigh nearly 1,000 lbs., and have a lengthy history of injuring animal keepers. And he had heard that a long time ago a keeper accidentally let a couple of zebras get out. It turned out to be a nightmare for a whole bunch of keepers that had to round them up. Then the negligent keeper was fired for causing such a dangerous situation. So with vigorous determination Jon took off after her, sloshing through the mud as the relentless rain slashed at his cheeks like icy needles.

As she approached the bighorn exhibit the wayward zebra paused to munch some tall green grass. In the midst of chasing after her, Jon stopped to pick up a 3-foot length of a 2" by 4" board that he found at the hay shed. Ever-so-slowly waving his arms and talking softly, he sauntered up to her and managed to turn the striped tormentor back around. Then foolishly, at great risk to himself, once she was headed the right way the desperate keeper abruptly swatted her with the board on that muscular rump. Jon was incredibly lucky that the zebra didn't kick him—it's their primary defense when lions jump up on their backside. She raced off instead, heading toward the night house, but abruptly stopped for yet another quick mouthful of grass. While the soles of his shoes gasped for air in the sodden mud, Jon plodded along and tapped her big butt again. He kept swatting her and she kept getting closer to the night house. She trotted straight back to the open gate, walked in, and Jon slammed the gate behind her. This time he made sure to secure the lock in the latch.

As he turned and trudged back to the truck, all of a sudden his nerves came on. Weary, chilled and thoroughly drenched, he didn't think he would ever stop trembling. At that point, the curator happened to drive by, wiper blades hacking wildly at the windshield. He rolled his window down, gave a hearty wave, and called out, "Everything under control, Jon?" Nodding assent, Jon flashed a big smile and waved goodbye, now thankful for the heavy rain and curator's keen sense of timing. Jon didn't share this adventure tale with anyone for several years.

About three years after Jon's incident, Matt also accidentally let a zebra out. And not just the one—he managed to let a second zebra out of its paddock, too.

There is an unwritten zoo rule about what to do if an animal gets out of its enclosure. In most cases the keeper should prop open the gate or door to allow the animal to find its way back in because more often than not that's what they will want to do. Escaped animals feel scared and disoriented, and usually want to go back to familiar territory.

Well, Matt's zebra had also flipped that same unsecured gate latch with her nose and took off. Shocked by the sight Matt panicked, but thankfully remembered to prop open the gate before he ran to try to head her back. Or maybe *not* so thankfully—in the mean time he had neglected to secure the *other* zebra. So of course she bolted out the open gate, too, and now Matt had two zebras to round up instead of one. With their unpredictable flightiness, this created a serious situation for zebras as well as keepers.

Fortunately, a long stretch of chain link fence abutted their paddock, so once Matt and a couple of other zookeepers got the zebras headed the right way slowly herding them back in was relatively easy. After the adventure ended, with quizzical authority Jon informed the keepers that it's simpler just to hit them in the butt with a 2" by 4"....

A Memorable Affair

That Pointers Sisters song *I'm So Excited* played around on a loop in my head. I felt jazzed, and really nervous, too, but anxious for this new experience. It was my first ever television appearance. The zoo's public relations director, Ned, had arranged for me to bring a hand-raised parrot to a local studio that broadcast a weekly live children's show. In his job as the zoo's photographer, Ned had a knack for capturing critters and employees in distinctive pictures. He also published a professional periodical for zoo members with a range of interesting articles to go with his delightful, artistic snapshots. Ned even managed an academic/journalistic appearance—slightly balding and sharp-eyed behind his black, square-framed glasses.

This day's TV segment starred "Papagayo," a handsome 4-year-old Amazon parrot with glossy, emerald green feathers. Bright red epaulets with a wisp of yellow adorned his wings. Only a slight sprinkling of yellow feathers mixed with the green ones on his head; once mature, he would wear a solid hood of intense yellow. A sweet disposition and tameness from being hand-raised made him perfect for education presentations. Papagayo had been someone's pet bird for a couple of years, before they decided that all the destructive chewing, shrill squawking, endless mess, and constant need for attention proved too much for their placid family home. Consequently, like so many exotic animals that confirm inappropriateness as pets, this parrot became a donation to the zoo.

So off the three of us went to The Gizmo Show in the zoo's small Datsun pickup truck. Because of the stick shift, Papagayo's transport crate wouldn't fit in the middle between Ned and me. And the seat wouldn't slide back far enough to allow the crate to sit on my lap. We couldn't put it in the bed of the truck either—it was so hot outside the asphalt would bake the soles of your shoes if you stood still too long. So I slid along the bench seat and sat next to Ned, stuffing the crate between the door and me. It made for a tight fit with my legs off to the side to avoid the stick shift, but it was the only option left for the 45-minute drive.

The show's host, "Gizmo," was a gangly, wild-looking caricature of a man reminiscent of *The Legend of Sleepy Hollow*'s Ichabod Crane. His colorful outfit looked like that of a 4-year-old allowed to choose his own wardrobe. He briefed us on where we should sit on the set, what time to expect to be on camera, and encouraged brief answers to the questions he would be asking. During the few moments before the show was to start, he asked about the bird quietly perched on my wrist. I had done my homework, and felt proud to be able to rattle off some fascinating facts. Moments later, the bubbly theme music began while the kids in the audience squealed and applauded—launching into his childish stunts and songs, Gizmo was on the air! While waiting for my moment of fame, I mentally reorganized the facts we had just discussed so that they were short, coherent, and geared for youngsters. Being so nervous, I feared I might make a fool of myself, and wanted to be prepared.

The opening stint soon finished and now the intense spotlights shined on Ned, Papagayo, and me. Gizmo plunked himself down on the bench alongside us. After he introduced Ned and me to the audience, I flashed a broad smile to the camera and enthusiastically introduced the parrot. The next words out of Gizmo's large, thin-lipped mouth formed a question that I was totally unprepared for, nothing at all that we had previously discussed. Nothing about the parrot, his native habitat, what foods he liked, or why he was so tame. Something logical. No, nothing at all like that. He asked, "So how many pounds of food does the zoo go through in a day?"

Totally dumbfounded by this unexpected subject, I fell speechless and stared straight ahead. Gizmo's question defied answering in a quick sentence. The zoo offers an infinite variety of food to our endless variety of critters: meat for the big cats, fish for pelicans, seeds for birds, monkey chow for primates, and rodents for snakes. We receive weekly deliveries of box after box of fresh produce piled high in a walk-in refrigerator that's as big as a bedroom. Refrigerated trucks arrive periodically with months' worth of frozen meats and fish that are hand-trucked into the equally large walk-in freezer. Cartons of crickets and mealworms are delivered each week by mail. Grain trucks fill huge hoppers at the loading dock a couple of times a month or so. A separate storage room holds stacks of sacks of seeds and other bagged foods. "How many pounds of food in a day?" It was impossible to calculate a response to that question!

Luckily Ned had appeared on the program many times before and, being the PR guy, didn't hesitate at all to come up with a sensible answer to such a broad question. I have no idea what he said. I just know how thankful I felt that he jumped into that vacuous dead-air space. Meanwhile I stared back at the camera lens with a silly grin, trying not to look as stupid as I felt.

While I tried to calm down and focus on Gizmo's next question, Papagayo decided that he didn't like the bright lights or all the unusual attention or who knows what. Maybe he sensed my discomfort. A complex metal framework supported a myriad of light fixtures and miles of electrical cables in the ceiling of that enormous studio. Among all this tangle of stuff the parrot spotted what he considered a better place to perch than my wrist, and, as my eyes widened and mouth gaped, off he went! He squawked raucously and circled over the kids' heads a few times, delighting the audience. Unaccustomed to flying, he beat his wings furiously, finally gaining enough altitude to land his pudgy body some twenty feet above us.

The bird's flight put an abrupt conclusion to the interview, and Ned and I patiently sat in the wings until the end of Gizmo's show. Once the crew shut off the spotlights and the audience left I easily coaxed Papagayo down onto my extended arm with a handful of his favorite treat of peanuts. Upset by all this adventure, he eagerly sought out the sanctuary of his crate.

Now that it was all over, as we returned to the zoo I could chuckle with Ned about the embarrassing events at the studio. It was late in the afternoon, quitting time for the keepers and gardeners. We drove up to the employee parking lot gate where a steady stream of cars came toward us. They were all leaving as we were arriving, and Ned had to pull the truck off to the side of the narrow road to let them through the gate.

Ned was on his way home within only fifteen minutes of our return and didn't know it yet, but he faced big trouble. When he walked in the door, his young wife stood there waiting, hands on hips. Sherry's wavy auburn hair framed her pretty face, and a serene and somewhat sly smile graced her lips. A well-meaning (?) zoo employee had wasted no time informing Sherry that Ned and I were "obviously" having an affair. And not only that, we were unabashedly blatant about it.

What we didn't realize while awaiting our turn to enter the zoo gate was that the people in the parade of oncoming cars couldn't see the parrot's crate jammed between the door and me. All they saw was Ned and I sitting shoulder to shoulder, laughing and having a good time. Fortunately, Sherry knew bet-

ter and Ned easily explained away the misconception. But she couldn't resist making him squirm. The whole sequence of the day's outrageous events became a great standing joke between the three of us.

Foxy Fennec Foxes

Sometimes a design flaw of an animal's exhibit can result in an escape at a zoo. Most enclosures include what we refer to as a "keeper safety." This simply means a vestibule between two doors so that the keeper always has a barrier while entering or exiting an exhibit. A safety that is visible to the public may tend to detract from a display's appearance, thus a designer may unwisely opt to omit it. An exhibit that looks attractive to the public can be an operational nightmare for keepers because of certain other unexpected design defects. This was the case at the zoo's fennec fox exhibit.

Among the smallest of the canid family, the fennec fox lives in the harsh deserts of northern Africa. Its diminutive face flaunts exceptionally oversized 6-inch-long ears that capture barely audible sounds and radiate excess heat. These beguiling little animals mate for life.

"I remember a couple of years ago when I accidentally let a fennec fox out of its exhibit," Rich told a group of keepers at break one morning. "I thought 'Fenwick' was in the night house already, but there he was, standing right next to the exhibit entry door when I opened it. There was no keeper safety back in those days, just the entrance door. And unfortunately, the way this stupid building was designed, there was no way for me to see into the night house to see if he was inside without first going into the exhibit.

"So anyway, as I opened the door," Rich continued, "the fox scooted right out between my feet and crawled into a gap in the rocks of the wall right near there. I stupidly reached in the hole and tried to grab him by the tail before he went down too far, but of course he turned around and started biting me. Luckily I had a big pair of leather gloves on the cart from when we had to take the eagle up to the vet, so I ran and got them. I grabbed him again, but even with gloves on, the whole time I had Fenwick by the tail he was biting the heck out of me. I didn't think I'd ever make it to the exhibit door with the fox before I'd lose my grip on him, but I managed to slip him back into the exhibit and shut the door just as he was wriggling free of my gloves."

Besides not having a keeper safety, this same fox exhibit had an open top. With its natural-looking gunite (sprayed concrete) walls and desert

landscaping, the display gave the appearance of a rugged box canyon. Up the hill a short way from the fox enclosure sat the Mandarin duck exhibit, consisting mostly of a rock-edged pond. It wasn't enclosed with any mesh, but instead only a 3-foot-high wall surrounded the display.

The male of the demure teal-sized Mandarin duck from Asia is considered among the most beautiful of all waterfowl. Early one summer, for some reason the exquisite little ducks began disappearing from their exhibit one by one without a trace. It became a frustrating mystery that continued for several nights. That is, until one morning when, of all places, the keeper found part of a Mandarin duck's little body in with the fennec foxes. Intrigued by this odd discovery, she searched around their exhibit a little more and found several piles of feathers and bones hidden under some thick shrubbery in a far back corner.

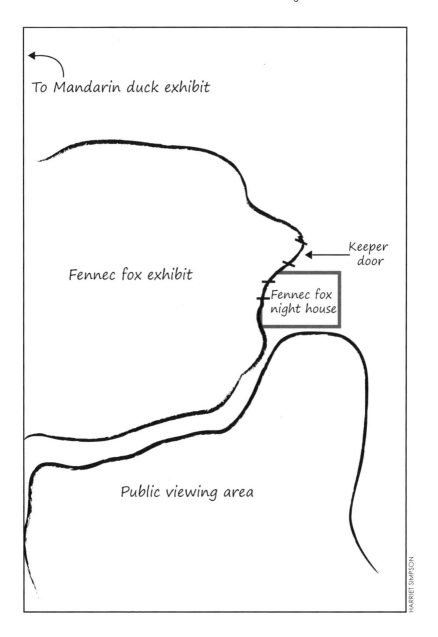

To Mandarin duck exhibit

Fennec fox exhibit

Keeper door

Fennec fox night house

Public viewing area

Evidently, each night one of the foxes somehow scaled the wall and hopped out the top of its display, ran up the hill and snatched a duck, then—in true devotion—returned to share the rich feast with its mate. And this one time, after so many nights in a row of duck on the menu, it seems they just couldn't eat another bite.

That afternoon the keepers trapped both the foxes and moved them to a temporary holding area. Meanwhile, the zoo architect made a quick review of the situation and came up with ideas for emergency alterations of the exhibit. The next day, the maintenance department installed a panel of mesh at the top of the rockwork, which interfered somewhat with the illusion of a box canyon, but nothing else could be done on such short notice. A few other quick exhibit modifications put an end to the crafty fox's nightly fine-dining excursions before no sweet little Mandarin ducks remained at all.

Sasha and the Clown

Menageries, precursors to modern zoological gardens, show up in history as early as the thirteenth century. Only royalty could afford to keep these "postage stamp collections," where one or maybe two individuals of different kinds of wondrous exotic animals existed in dismal conditions for their short, tragic lives. Menageries morphed into zoos, with sterile exhibition of animals in tiny and barren concrete enclosures that allowed for easy cleaning and heavy bars obstructing viewing by the public. Zoos have matured dramatically, especially in the past forty years or so, focusing more on recreating natural habitats and providing behavioral enrichment.

Back in the 1960s, the children's section of the zoo hosted birthday parties and on cool summer evenings put on trained animal shows. The two biggest stars included a baby elephant and an endearing little 2-year-old chimpanzee named "Sasha." Keepers dressed her in a silly clown costume with big, multicolored polka dots and floppy hat. And, of course, the people that ran these shows thought it would be real cute to have the chimp's keeper dressed in a matching clown suit. Alan, at a lanky 6'4" and barely 160 lbs., had a somewhat comical appearance even without the colorful outfit.

One balmy evening Sasha and Alan, clad in their clown attire, walked hand in hand to the show arena. Alan didn't hear or see anything unusual but suddenly something spooked the chimp. She yanked her hand from Alan's and took off running in a loping gait. Then she rocketed straight up to the top of a tall palm tree. Sasha was a sweet little chimp and well trained, but quite naive, and something had really scared her. And now she sat alone and terrified up in this unfamiliar setting, and had no idea what to do next.

Alan turned ashen while grabbing at his nauseated stomach as he watched Sasha scamper away from him. He had only been a keeper for a

CINDY BARRY

couple of months at this, his very first job. He feared the little chimp might get hurt and, even though he couldn't really be blamed, felt sure he would get in serious trouble for the incident. Alan yelled to someone from the nearby snack bar to keep an eye on the chimp, that he'd be right back. He dashed down to the commissary kitchen at the back of the zoo for some fruit to lure her out of the tree.

What must zoo visitors have thought when they saw this stilt-legged, gangly clown in polka dots sprinting through the zoo with long strides, clutching an armload of bananas, apples and grapes? Alan was too concerned about getting Sasha safely down to be embarrassed at the time. It turned out to be pretty easy to coax the chimp from her lofty perch because she would do anything for grapes. And Alan's easy manner, reassuring voice, and comforting arms held much more appeal to Sasha than trying to balance high up on the spindly palm fronds with their hooked and slashing edges.

Eventually, the zoo considered these kinds of trained animal shows to be demeaning to the animals and phased them out. Education became the predominant theme. This part of the zoo still offers a big playground with picnic tables for birthday party activities, but no one can recall what ever happened to those goofy, made-to-order clown outfits worn by keeper and chimp in the old days.

Going for the Throat

angerous animals at a zoo usually have a holding yard and/or indoor quarters separate from their exhibit. Zookeepers use a transfer door to shift them from one space to the other. These separate quarters give the animals a place to spend the night away from any public access, and create a safe situation for keepers while they complete daily chores in the exhibit. Sometimes, however, skittish or obstinate animals refuse to cooperate in the transfer, leaving a keeper vulnerable.

Such was the case with Jim and a pair of white-handed gibbons. These 12-lb. apes from the forests of Asia are incredibly loud for their petite size. Their ghostly, bubbling duets sung at sunrise can be heard as far as a mile away (a loud voice is essential when living in dense jungle). Spending all their time swinging about in trees, gibbons have squat legs and disproportionately long arms and buff shoulders, making them the quickest and most agile of the primates. Distrustful, flighty, and often obstinate, gibbons cause great consternation for keepers. They sport alarmingly large canine teeth. These little apes are sneaky—you'll never see an attack coming. They wait until you look away or turn your back, and move so fast that one can pounce on you, bite, and then spring away before you even realize what's happening.

This particular pair of gibbons persistently refused to go into their night house and the male always acted exceptionally high-strung and unpredictable. So every day, Jim hosed the floor of their exhibit while keeping a constant eye on him. It was probably inevitable that the devious ape would some day attack him, but this one morning seemed no different than any other. The gibbon leapt onto the wary keeper's back the moment Jim finished hosing and turned to leave, savagely biting into the flimsy flesh of his neck. Before he had a chance to react, those nasty big canines sliced through on either side of Jim's jugular. Fortunately the bite went deeper than the vein and the teeth closed *behind* it—failing, just barely, to puncture the blood vessel. This kind of traumatic event can radically shake a keeper's confidence. Jim gave his two weeks notice later that afternoon and never went in with the gibbons again for the remainder of his time there.

———

One pair of gibbons I only occasionally worked with lived on a small island and there was no way to convince them to be locked into their night house either. The old male, "Jocko," had sleek black hair and eyes beginning to cloud with cataracts. He was so congenial that he and Zeke, his regular keeper, would lie on the grass and sunbathe together. Not so with "Jo," the tempestuous female gibbon. For some reason (maybe because she was blonde) Jo seemed to have a particular hatred for female keepers with blonde hair. She behaved pretty well with anyone else (Zeke was blonde). Being blonde myself, her prejudice always left a despairing knot in my stomach any time I had to interact with the gibbons.

The sprinkler system on Gibbon Island sprang a serious leak one intensely hot day, but Zeke wasn't around to help out. So three maintenance guys and I rowed over in the boat to repair the plumbing. My sole job was to keep the two gibbons—especially Jo— at bay so the men could safely work, a grave responsibility. Jocko caused no problems at all, quietly sitting ever watchful at the top of the tallest palm tree, as far away from us as he could get. He hugged himself with those long arms for reassurance. Jo, on the other hand, exceedingly agitated, swung continually through the trees and on the ropes. Her loud whoops sounded like an obnoxious, incessant car alarm. My woeful armaments seemed insignificant: A hose (not much help at the point when the water supply had to be turned off) and a net on an extension pole to threateningly wave around. Thankfully, she never got close enough for me to have to use them more than a couple of times.

That searing sun hung belligerently high in the sky, looking like a hard-boiled egg yolk. Were the trickles of water running down my back caused by the heat or my nerves? I couldn't tell. After what seemed like hours even though it was more likely just thirty minutes, the crew finally finished and all went without incident. With a final spray of the restored water from the hose I coaxed Jo to move her farthest from us. As we began our departure from the island the men piled into the boat except for one who intended to push us off. It was my turn to board. At the very moment when I took my eyes off Jo and turned to step into the boat she somehow instantly transported herself from there to here. She attacked with a lightning-fast glancing wallop. I can still feel the hard thud of her body slamming into my back, and then the powerful push-off with her short, springy legs.

In that meteoric moment the malicious gibbon ripped my chambray work shirt and her fingernails deeply scratched the skin on the ribs of my chest. Her toenails gouged into my back, drawing blood there as well. And I could feel Jo's face buried at the nape of my neck in my long hair. I cringed and bent over in reaction to her frenzied biting. Before bounding away, all she got was a mouthful of hair and shirt collar, which now had puncture holes from those savage canines.

That did it for me. Gibbons always made me nervous anyway and I made a point never to go back to that island. I considered saving the evidentiary shirt, but it felt more cathartic to throw it away. In the end, that little brat got her way, for no blonde female keepers are allowed to set foot on Jo's island.

Young reticulated giraffe. At birth, giraffes are already the
height of a human.

Nothing to It

Another time at the morning break, Ben related a few incidents of animals being out of place that weren't his fault but were absurdly easy situations to remedy.

"One day I was walking past the giraffes' outdoor holding pen on the way to my work area," Ben said, "and I thought to myself, Something doesn't look right with the giraffe over there. So I walked towards him and as I got closer I realized that he was standing on the wrong side of the fence—not *in* the paddock, you know, but *behind* it! It was the big male, who was pretty docile, but still could easily spook. He was all antsy, and looking around like something was making him nervous."

As long as you are quiet and slow moving around giraffes they are quite placid to work with. An adult male reticulated giraffe weighs in at 1½ tons and has a correspondingly massive 25-lb. heart. He stands an astounding 18 feet tall on 6-foot-long legs. Just imagine—an average-sized man could stand between the front legs under a male giraffe's chest! Striking out with those stilt legs is part of their defense against lions, with the sharp-edged hooves inflicting serious damage.

"So what'd you do?" asked Janie.

"Well, I circled the long way around," Ben continued, "and saw that somehow the gate to his paddock had been left partially open. Apparently after the giraffe walked out he couldn't figure out how to get back in. So I propped the gate wide open, circled back behind him and kinda casually strolled along, slowly guiding him back into the paddock. There was nothing to it, you know, but my heart was in my throat the entire time. It was stupid of me to handle this situation by myself, but I didn't think I had time to find anyone to help. I never did find out how the gate got left open to begin with."

"Another day," said Ben, "I was driving along on my golf cart and happened to look up the side road toward the service gate of the rhino exhibit. I looked back to the road I was driving on to continue, but thought to myself that something funny was going on up that way. I stopped the cart, backed up a bit, and looked up there again but this time everything looked fine. As I started to move on, I still felt something was odd, and so I looked back again. It was just something I sensed, you know?

"This time, I caught a glimpse of the same thing I'd gotten an inkling of the first time. It was the male rhino's head as he took a step out through the open service gate! Then it went back behind the wall. Then Mubu would peek out again. I found out later that someone had interrupted the keeper during his routine, and, planning to return, he drove off without shutting the gate. Later, when he shifted the rhinos from their night house out onto display, he'd completely forgotten about it. From inside the night house you can't see the gate, so he couldn't see that it was still open."

Janie asked, "Why do you think Mubu didn't leave the paddock?"

"Rhino's are supposed to have such bad vision, I guess Mubu just wasn't sure enough of what he was seeing to brave venturing all the way out. He'd just drift out a couple of steps, then move back, then out, and back. It was another case of me being alone in a dangerous situation with no time to solicit help. But shooing this 12-foot-long animal with 2½ tons of bulk back in and shutting the gate was surprisingly easy. It was funny, I just talked to him real quiet as I approached to the side and gently moved my arms. Mubu actually seemed relieved not to have this big decision-making dilemma: Should I go, or should I stay; should I go, or…?"

A Matter of Trust

Teamwork is a critically important aspect of keepers who work with dangerous animals. Like soldiers, they need to be able to trust that their coworkers know what to do and won't hesitate to jump in to help in a risky situation. In this job you may spend most of your time working alone, but in some situations and especially during a crisis, teamwork is essential.

One way that a zoo can display a bird in a large, open exhibit is to clip the primary (long, outermost) feathers of only one wing. Then, if the bird tries to fly, it's too off balance and ends up spiraling right back down to the ground. Periodically, of course, the bird molts its feathers and grows new ones, so keepers have to stay vigilant and re-clip those primaries. Some of the larger birds, such as storks and cranes, have such a big wingspan that even with one side clipped they may still manage labored flight on a windy day.

Early one stormy afternoon, a Ruppell's griffon vulture caught a brisk breeze and soared easily over the 8-foot fence of the sprawling African savannah exhibit. It was something we watched for on rare, blustery days. Fortunately a gardener spotted the bewildered bird standing in the road next to the exhibit. She radioed me and kept her in sight until Joe and I showed up with nets and a crate.

Handling a vulture, especially a sizable, strong one such as the Ruppell's, can be tricky. They weigh as much as a bowling ball and measure nearly 3 feet long beak-to-tail with an incredible 8-foot wingspan. (In comparison, an average adult man's arms span about 6 feet, fingertip to fingertip.) With hawks and eagles, getting the legs under immediate control is crucial. Their toes wield long, sharp talons used to grasp and pierce prey. Vultures, however, have comparatively weak feet and short, not-so-sharp talons. But their powerful curved beak and strong neck muscles are formidable. These adaptations allow them to quickly rend pieces of meat off a carcass amongst the fierce competition of other vultures and scavengers like jackals and vicious hyenas.

When Joe and I arrived we found the escapee crouching under a bush alongside a fence, so getting her into a net proved relatively easy. Extricating her from the mesh to slip her into the crate, though, gave us a bit of a challenge, but Joe managed his job perfectly. As I gingerly untangled her from the net he restrained her powerful wings by wrapping his body and arms around the bird, meanwhile clutching her kicking legs with his hand. Once her writhing head was just about free from the net I made a grab for it, but instead snatched the vulture's long, skinny neck just below the jaw.

She continuously wriggled her head around, just like an unmanned garden hose with a knife attached to the end, snaking wildly under full water pressure. I thought that I had that muscular neck fully extended and under control, but it didn't take long to see how wrong I was. The vulture had just a bit more unexpected stretch left. I couldn't believe it when I saw her head immediately telescope up and she reached to bite the closest thing to her face—Joe's cheek. With a violent twist she made contact, the hooked beak slitting his skin in a neat circular slice. Luckily, it turned out to be somewhat of a glancing blow, with Joe's coarse beard offering a minimal layer of interference. If the bird had aimed just a bit lower and been more direct, she could have ripped right into Joe's jugular vein in his neck. Had she been higher in his arms he could have lost an eye. Even though he survived the incident rattled but relatively unscathed, I'm sure it scuttled Joe's confidence in working with me in future animal-handling situations.

One winter day an unusually strong windy storm blew into the area. Standing with wings outstretched at the top of the hill in the African savannah exhibit, the male Ruppell's vulture took advantage of a brisk gust. He gracefully soared over the fence and alighted on the rooftop of a conveniently nearby building, the night house of another exhibit. This did not go unnoticed by the occupant of that exhibit—the female lion! At first the majestic vulture stood proudly, surveying all from his wondrous new vantage point, until he realized

TOM BLACKLEDGE

his dilemma. Then, trying to act nonchalant, he preened his feathers nonstop in nervous displacement activity while the lioness paced and stalked from below. She never took her eyes off him.

It was out of the cat's routine to be asked to come inside the night house during the middle of the day, but through persistence the keepers managed to coax the lion inside while other keepers formed a simple plan for rescuing the bird. The lucky adventurer had easily made it over the veldt fence, but if he hadn't gotten enough lift to make it to that roof he most certainly would have become an unexpected lunch treat for the flabbergasted feline. The next time he may not be so lucky.

DICK GEORGE

When hand-raising chicks of cavity-nesting birds like these red-breasted toucans we discovered a neat trick: Lay a folded towel over the top of the box, leaving a portion uncovered. When ready to offer food, draw the fold across to darken the box interior and then immediately withdraw it again. This simulates the brief darkening of the nest entrance as the adult arrives with food. Though their eyes aren't open yet they sense the change, which stimulates the chicks to beg.

Notice the "hinged" tail? It gets crowded in the confines of the nest cavity with developing long beaks and tails, so the chick turns his head and rests his beak across his back. Then to prevent damage to the developing pinfeathers the tail flips up over his head making the nestling a tidy little ball. See the book cover photo for these toucan chicks nearly ready to fledge.

DICK GEORGE

Tiny Tidbits

The following is an assemblage of small snippets of interesting animal behaviors or surprising things that can happen at a zoo without warning.

One sunny afternoon one of the zoo gardeners approached me with a concerned expression on her face. She told me that she had just seen Ron with the Australian black swan cygnets and he was acting in a peculiar way. Ron was one of our most reliable "relief" keepers, trained in several different work areas to fill in when another keeper called in sick or went on vacation. The baby swans were part of the group of animals that he was assigned to that day in the Children's Zoo. The gardener said that Ron was sitting on the edge of their little pond, playfully slapping the water. And he was talking to the cygnets like they were toys, as if he was a 4-year-old.

As I approached the pond, indeed he was perched there on the edge grinning broadly, splashing, and pronouncing with childish glee how cute the babies looked. The cygnets were undeniably adorable fluffy gray balls of downy feathers, about the size of grapefruit. But this behavior was certainly out of character for Ron. What we didn't know was that he happened to be a diabetic. As we chatted, I managed to coax Ron to relate some of his health situation to me. Because I was somewhat familiar with the effects of diabetes I realized that his glucose level had dropped too low. He needed sugar in his blood fast.

Australian black swan and cygnets.

I immediately called on the radio for anyone available to bring oranges, soda, or candy bars, whatever they could find the quickest, and get down to the Children's Zoo, pronto!

Fortunately, this particular incident ended up harmless to keeper and animals. But imagine if Ron had been working with the lions or orangutans that day, and in clouded judgment due to his medical condition went into their enclosure to play with them....

In another incident, while driving home from the zoo one day a snack bar employee happened to notice a diabetic coworker innocently driving down the wrong side of a divided road. Fortunately he was able to intercept her before anything disastrous happened.

Even though an employee's medical information is private, some zoos may require that coworkers be notified of serious conditions such as diabetes and epilepsy. Safety may be more important than privacy when a health situation might put the lives of the individual, animals, fellow employees, and/or the public at risk.

One morning I became distracted while refilling the small pond I'd just cleaned in the superb starling exhibit. The water began to overflow the edges, flooding a nearby mouse hole. As I bent down to turn off the hose, the soaked and frantic occupant swam out of his hole and raced for the closest high and dry hiding spot he could find, which happened to be up the inside of my pant leg. I'm glad no witnesses were around to be entertained by my spontaneous dance performance....

If you ever prune a branch only to find that there's a hummingbird nest woven onto it, immediately find a way to tie it back on as close to the original position as you can! Even if the eggs or chicks may not have survived the fall the mother may nest again on the same spot (they've been known to use an old nest site the following year). Also, sometimes people are positive that the mother has abandoned the chicks of a nest they've been watching outside their window, but more than likely that's not true. Well-meaning, they cut the branch and bring the precious cargo to the zoo, but that may not be a good idea unless the chicks are obviously suffering distress.

Hand-raising hummer chicks challenges even the most dedicated keeper. A miniscule crop (handy storage pouch between mouth and stomach) coupled with a high metabolic rate commands feeding about every 15 minutes from sunup to sundown. A mere tiny drop at a time of sugar water mixed with protein powder is the easy part—it's those fruit flies that can be exasperating.

It may surprise some people to learn that besides flower nectar hummingbirds consume a great many tiny insects like gnats and fruit flies. This essential source of protein and roughage must be provided to the chicks for them to develop properly. Hummer babies don't gape their mouth open like a robin nestling, so the insects can't just be stuffed down the throat. The chicks repeatedly stick that long tongue up into the eyedropper to sip the protein/sugar water, so there's no easy way to get that miniscule bug into them. I have tried putting them in the nectar but they float then stick to the inside of the dropper. A fruit fly might end up on the edge of the beak, but then just cling there, out of range of that rigid tongue (it's leaner than a toothpick and stiff, like a thin fingernail). It can't be licked off.

Any time I hand-raised hummer chicks I would take them home on my weekend, setting them up in the easier-to-clean bathroom (the liquid that gets put in the front end goes out the back end later in a surprisingly strong squirt). One time I just happened to be present when one of the youngsters took his maiden flight. As much a surprise to him I think as to me, he flew *backwards* about five feet, gave a loud squeak, then crash-landed right into my neck and tangled in my long hair.

Experts don't advise artificial feeding of wild adult hummingbirds because the continuous presence of food may interrupt their natural migration

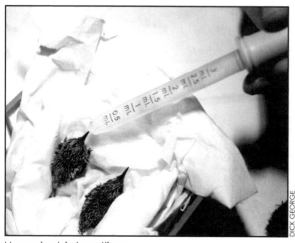

Hummingbird nestlings.

movement. But if you do decide to provide them with a feeder never offer honey (it causes a fungus fatal to hummers). Some other tips: You don't need to pay for expensive "nectar" mixes—in fact, the red dye ingredient can damage the bird's liver. Just offer sugar water, using four parts water to one part sugar. Bring the water to a boil, dissolve the sugar in it, and let the mixture cool before filling. Keep the feeder scrupulously clean and well rinsed, and hang it in the shade. Better yet, plant a plethora of their favorite flowers instead—especially red or purple tubular flowers such as penstemon, columbine, and hummingbird bush (your nursery can help suggest what grows best in your area). Maybe a hummingbird will find your yard so bountiful she will raise a nestful of babies there.

"No! Stop!! Don't drink that water!!!"

Indeed, that glistening water did look cool and refreshing as it trickled gaily over the rocks on such a hot day. But I was dumbfounded and screeched my cart to a stop as I drove by the scene. Under the approving eye of her mother, a young girl placed an empty soda cup under the spilling water as it exited under a wall surrounded by lush masses of flowering bushes. I thought at first she was just going to use it to splash on her legs to cool off, but watched in horror as she raised the cup to her lips. I probably scarred mother and daughter for life with my shrill remonstration!

The attractive streams and lakes on the zoo grounds were put to good use, routing the water through one exhibit after another for a multitude of animals: flamingos, tapirs, capybara, mountain lion, numerous varieties of monkeys, and many more critters. Not to mention the hordes of migratory waterfowl that showed up on the lakes each winter. The cumulative concentration of contaminants from all this wildlife must be staggering by the time the water reaches the alligator pond, just on the other side of that pretty wall, before exiting the zoo. I still gag when I think of what could have happened to this little girl if she'd drunk that foul and bilious water.

⁌————⁌

At the edge of the dark, still pond rimmed with cattails and rugged boulders in a remote area of the zoo a handsome wild wood rat sat back on his haunches, nose twitching, as if he sensed something. Then his nimble little paws resumed the vigorous cleaning of his face and shiny pelage. Young and naïve, he seemed oblivious to my electric golf cart as I silently rolled up near the shore. I took a few moments to enjoy watching his activities in this tranquil nature scene.

Just as I was about to resume my journey the rodent suddenly vanished from view. What the heck just happened? I didn't see him scamper off. I pulled the cart up a foot or so and there he was, just behind the nearby palm tree—snatched in the jaws of a fat and glistening gopher snake. The predator immediately wrapped its steely muscular body around the hapless victim, forbidding him the chance to inhale. So perfect was the snake's camouflage that neither the rodent nor I ever noticed him—a fatal mistake for Mr. Rat and a heady educational opportunity for me.

⁌————⁌

Nesting season for many of the zoo's bird species was imminent, so I dug around in the big barrel of fresh bark chips at the back of the zoo to fill my bucket. I intended to drive around to the various aviaries to replenish the supply of nest material in the boxes in time for egg laying. Ouch, what was that on my shin? It felt like a hot needle poking me. When I rubbed my pant leg below my knee, I felt it again, but thought nothing more of it.

As I drove around on the cart that spot on my shin began to hurt. And then really hurt. I diverted from my plan and headed for the zoo hospital where the vet took a look at the bright red, quarter-size spot that had developed on the site. He told me to go home and pack my leg in ice, informing me that I'd been stung by a bark scorpion, the smallest variety of scorpion but one with a particularly potent venom.

By the time I got home the pain had spread to include my leg from the knee to my toes so I did exactly as the vet recommended. After a while though, hunger pangs convinced me I needed to fix some dinner. And anyway, being pretty thoroughly numbed, my leg didn't hurt quite as much anymore, so I figured I didn't need to lie around in bed any more. Before I'd rummaged in the kitchen very long though, I discovered just how essential that ice had been and couldn't get back to the ice packs fast enough. I had to settle for a handful of crackers to eat.

At the incident's maximum, my entire leg all the way to the top of my hip was involved with the sharp, constant pain. It took only about 24 hours for it to gradually reverse and subside back down to the original spot on my shin, but that quarter-sized spot surrounding the punctures stayed sore and red for months after.

⌒

One day a local wildlife rescue organization called the zoo asking if we might have room to house a Harris hawk that had been injured so badly she could never be returned to the wild. We happened to have a male on display that was perfectly fine, so we jumped at the chance for a unique opportunity. Our healthy Harris hawk got released back to the wild, and the injured bird got a second chance at life on exhibit at the zoo. We installed an educational graphics panel to explain that her perpetually droopy wing was not functional because the humerous bone had been irreparably shattered.

In the photo at the end of the Preface of this book you'll find the zoo's male Harris hawk at the apex of being tossed up into the air on release. What you don't know is that immediately after the picture was taken he unceremoniously flopped to the ground and just sat there, dumbfounded at his new situation. We were ecstatic when he took wing to follow another Harris hawk we released moments after him, a rehabilitated female. A game and fish warden made us even happier when he informed us that he spotted the two hawks still together a month later.

A Loss of Bravado

B en and Rich enjoyed working together as keepers for many years. Even after Rich left the zoo to attend vet school he would occasionally return to visit and talk about old times, entertaining the keepers who hadn't heard the stories.

"Compared to me, Ben, you sure had a better safety record. Do you remember the first time anything out of the ordinary happened while you were a keeper?" Rich asked.

"Oh sure," Ben chuckled. "There was an incident just a couple of months after I started working here. The only animals I ever had get out on me were the two young gorillas, 'Flora' and 'Mango.' They were about 4 and 6 years old, like little kids and really devoted to each other. They would wrestle and tumble, and snuggle when sleeping—those two did everything together. They always rattled and banged on the doors to make noise in their play. This one day they accidentally broke a latch and slid open the keeper door to their night house.

"I happened to walk into the building and step into the hall just when they slipped out of their room. I had a big armload of fresh hay to replace their bedding and all of a sudden the gorilla's door just glided open in front of me and, out they came! They just walked out hand in hand, and we're all three standing there in the hall together. I was so shocked I stupidly yelled,

'What the hell are you doing out here?!'"

Rich asked, "What did you do to get them back?"

"I tried juggling the hay real quick to one arm so I could pull the entrance door shut behind me, but Mango was so quick he was already outside, leading Flora along by the hand. Mango was older and could be a little aggressive sometimes, so I didn't really trust him. But Flora still acted more like a big baby. The only thing I could see close by was a bamboo rake, so I tossed the hay aside and grabbed the rake, and tried nudging Mango back inside with it. But he snatched it from me and, off he went. And that was it! I couldn't believe what just happened. Luckily, when Mango grabbed the rake he let go of Flora. She actually seemed relieved to see me and let me hold her hand, so I just led her back to their room.

"Meanwhile the zoo had opened about a half hour before," Ben continued, "and a big school group of probably fifty noisy kids came up the hill toward the exhibit, yelling and running all over the place. Suddenly Mango realized he was out in unknown territory, all alone, and here was this noisy bunch of humans all headed right for him. He tossed the rake up in the air and ran screaming back inside and down the hall, banging on the door to get back in with Flora. Of course I was very happy to oblige."

Rich said, "Don't you wish all these kinds of things ended that easily?!"

Is Anybody Listening?

"Y ou know, for all the years I've worked at the zoo, I never got hurt by my own stupid mistakes," Rich mentioned to a bunch of keepers one evening at a favorite bar. "I've been kicked by a kangaroo, rammed by a bighorn sheep, nipped by a fennec fox, and even bitten by the big male orangutan 'Bo.' And I had that guy to deal with that jumped into the exhibit to "ride" the rhino. But those incidents all happened when I was being extremely careful, you know? Just doing my regular job, my routine, and then something went wrong."

"That must've been horrifying when Bo grabbed you," Ben said. "He had you by the hair didn't he, had your head up against the bars?"

"Oh man, he sure did," Rich replied. "This was in the old orang exhibit where there was only about a 3-foot-wide keeper walkway between the bars and the wall of their night quarters. You never saw that old building because you started working here right after it was torn down. It was a terrible design. Anyway, I'd been told that the bars were close enough together that the orangs couldn't get their big hands through. Back then, Bo wasn't as huge as he is now, but he still weighed about 180 lbs. Bo has tried to grab at me lots of times because for some reason he's always wanted to get hold of the hose. I guess because he has never been able to have it, you know, and it looks intriguing. Also, I could interact somewhat safely with the other two orangs 'Myrna' and 'Frodo,' who was just a baby at the time, so he'd get real jealous. But anyway, I guess Bo's been so frustrated with me that he makes a point to try to grab at me any time I walk by.

"Well, I'd never seen him get his big hands through any further than just the fingers, but apparently there was this one area at the bottom corner of the bars that on that day he discovers is just a little bit wider. So he manages to slip his hand and arm through up to his elbow. There's lots of visitors outside the window watching me feed Myrna and Frodo some pieces of fruit. I happen to step back and turn Bo's way just as he thrusts his arm through that space and he's able to grab my shirt and jerk me off balance toward him. And man, instantly, it's the most scared I've ever been in my life. My knees got real weak, but I knew I couldn't give in to him. I had to keep alert and try to think one step ahead of him.

"So then Bo's other hand is immediately on my head, pulling my hair. My face is so close to his face I can smell his banana breath. He starts to smash the top of my head up against the bars, and just by my reflexes I put my hands out to break the impact. I feel my hands hit the bars, and, I can't see, but all of a sudden on the thumb of my right hand I notice something that feels warm, soft and mushy, and I realize it's a tongue. And then I remember that one time Bo bit off the end of one of Tom's index fingers, you know, the guy that used to work here when the zoo first opened up.

"So anyway as soon as I realize it's a tongue, and it's Bo's, I panic and start trying to pull my hand back, and, it's all like slow motion. He's still got a tight grip on my hair, and I can feel his teeth come down as I'm pulling my thumb out of his mouth. There's this perfectly square groove being cut in my thumb by his front tooth, going deeper and deeper. It starts at the far end joint and just keeps getting deeper to where it took out my fingernail, but didn't get into any bone. So I set my feet to get good balance and yanked my hands off. And then he was just holding me by my hair against the bars. I was so terrified I didn't even feel any pain in my finger, but there was blood everywhere.

"What were you thinking just then?" Ben asked. "How were you going to get away from him?"

"It's funny," Rich said, "but my first thought was, anything you give to those orangs it seems like they peel. You give them a tire to play in and they peel the tread off. They steal a hose from you, they peel it. You give them palm fronds and they peel them into strips of fiber. Everything they get, they peel. So I'm thinking Bo's gonna bite a hole in my head and peel my scalp off. He's gonna peel me alive! That's my first thought. And I say to myself, Okay, I need to stay calm, but I gotta do something really quick or this is it. I figure in my mind I have about thirty seconds before I get peeled like a banana in front of all these people.

"I happened to have a cigarette lighter in my pocket, even though I don't smoke. I figured if I ever got in trouble in some exhibit I could always light a fire, even if I had to pull a shirt off and set it on fire. I always wondered, What if I'm down in the tiger moat cleaning and someone stupidly puts the tigers out, doesn't know I'm there? Maybe I'd have a chance to keep the cats away from me by starting a fire, or I could light a signal fire, so I always carried that lighter.

"So I start to reach into my pocket for it. Every time I do, Bo pulls me by the hair and slams my head against the bars with both hands: BAM! BAM! There's a broom about five feet away, and I can't quite reach it with my hand or foot, but every time I try to stretch toward it, he's BAM! BAM! my head again. Bo has wanted to get me real bad for a real long time, but he's so shocked to finally have his hands on me, I think it's like, 'I got him! I got him! But what do I do now?' And every time I try to make any kind of move…BAM! BAM!

"I also carry a pocketknife, but my first choice is the lighter, just to hold it up. But I can't get into my pocket. Second choice is the broom—can't reach it. Third choice is the knife. I'm going to see if maybe I can just reach out and poke him with it enough to make him let go—not a blade, just the pocketknife itself—but he still won't let me get in my pockets. So I think, okay, there's a bucket of food over there. I'm going to ask someone in the crowd to throw a rock through the window. Maybe the noise will scare him. If it doesn't, maybe they can throw some fruit in to him."

Ben asked, "Were the people aware that you were in trouble or did they just stand there watching?"

"I talked to a lot of the people right afterwards," Rich said. "And it's something that happens—you're not sure if it's real or a joke or what. Some people thought it was real and went running for help. Some thought it was funny and said, 'Hey, come here and look at this!' Because there were plenty of times I'd go in there and Myrna and Frodo would 'mug' me. They'd go through my pockets for treats and tug on my beard. Everyone thought it was cute and you'd stand there and put on a show.

"So anyway, I'm bent over, looking at my feet, and Bo's got a hold of me by the hair. The first time I say real loud, 'Would somebody please throw a rock through the window?' and there's dead silence. Ten seconds pass and I yell a little louder, 'Would somebody please throw a rock through the window?' There's a big mob of people out there, so I know they can hear me. But after the second time and still nothing happens, I finally yell, "Damn it, somebody throw a God damn rock through the window!' And all of a sudden I hear this explosion of glass. Bo jumps back, letting go of my hair, and I step away. And it's over."

"Did you ever find out who threw the rock?" Ben asked.

"I spoke to the guy afterwards and he was one of the ones who thought I was just messing around until I started swearing."

"We haven't had anything exciting like that happen at the zoo in a real long time," Ben commented. "I guess that must be because you left!"

Baby Moon Beauty

You are undoubtedly familiar with the glorious beauty of the male peacock. They're so commonplace often no one gives them a second look. But have you ever scrutinized the detail of the feather patterns up close? Especially when the male looks most striking, with the tail spread like a fan during his breeding display. It's not just the "eyes" on the well-known long tail plumes; the small feathers blanketing the upper tail (known as tail coverts) are exquisitely intricate as well. Unique details of partial designs of each individual feather combine to make a strikingly pretty pattern over his back when the tail's not raised. But as the tail is erected during a display the coverts overlap and patterns merge to create a different stunning design. The iridescent blue feathers adorning his head glisten with a silvery bright sheen in the sunlight. Near his eyes, black stripes of miniature feathers contrast sharply with the white facial skin that's naked. Don't forget, of course, those outrageous half-dozen or so dainty filoplumes on delicate stems bobbling on top of his head, finishing off that fashionable look.

As I drove my cart past the zoo office one day, I noticed a free-roaming peacock displaying in all his grandeur. There wasn't a drab female anywhere in the vicinity to impress, but in his brain was something even more stimulating. With single-minded intensity, he repeatedly shimmered his tail at his own reflection in a truck's baby moon hubcap. The hollow quills audibly vibrated as he shook. With each shimmer he leaned a half step forward, dipping down in a curtsy to exaggerate the performance. One can only imagine how the bird perceived his expanded "fish-eye" image from the convex shape of the shiny hubcap.

On my return about an hour later the peacock was still there, mesmerized by the majesty of his reflection and continuing his pageantry with unwavering determination. I wondered if he had managed to find the "three other competitors" surrounding the vehicle.

So when that truck finally drove away wouldn't you like to know if the bird felt disappointed not to be able to admire himself anymore, or did he believe he had finally succeeded in driving off a particularly handsome rival?

Edema Enigma

W hile at home finishing up the dinner dishes one night, I got a panicky call from Dick, the evening keeper. He said that "Meru," the 8-year-old female tiger, limped a bit on her right front paw when she entered the night quarters about an hour before. Now the foot was noticeably swollen and she was pacing, but wouldn't put any weight on it at all. Agitated and growling constantly, she seemed to be in a lot of discomfort.

I told Dick that I'd call and consult with the veterinarian and, because I lived only 2 miles from the zoo, would meet him at the tiger exhibit in about 15 minutes. Kendall, the zoo's veterinarian, who lived 45 minutes away, suspected a possible break somewhere in Meru's foot or leg. She said she'd swing by a colleague's office to pick up some portable x-ray equipment on her way in. (Back in those days the zoo's veterinary office contained a woefully minimal amount of equipment.)

By the time I arrived at the tiger exhibit Meru's foot had swollen hugely. There was nothing Dick and I could do except anxiously watch her and wait for the vet. Although probably only a little more than another hour passed, the wait seemed interminable. Now the cat's entire leg was involved as well. She couldn't stand and the growling had turned to pathetic moans. It was obvious by the time Kendall arrived that there was no need for the x-ray equipment after all—Meru had suffered a rattlesnake bite.

The foot looked elephantine, Meru drooled profusely, and she was obviously in shock. Her lymph nodes worked furiously, trying in vain to combat the effects of the snake's hemotoxic venom, which destroys tissues, disrupts blood clotting, and can degenerate organs. While the vet immobilized the tiger with a tranquilizer dart so we could safely go in with her, I raced

CINDY BARRY

up to a nearby community hospital to get a supply of antivenin that she called in. Would medicine based on horse serum and made for humans work on a tiger? And how much should be administered? Worse yet, what should we do if Meru had an allergic reaction to the drug as sometimes happens with humans? What if it didn't work at all, what should we try next?

With these questions in mind, we really had no choice but to administer the drug. Meru's foot had grown huge with grotesque distortion, the claws completely hidden in the folds of her bloated toes. Her leg was distended all the way up into the shoulder. It was hard to imagine that the limb could balloon to such enormity. Even more incredulous, the pads of her corpulent foot were covered with tiny drops of clear liquid constantly beading up, joining together and dripping, then being replaced with new beads. With all the internal pressure on her tissues the lymph fluid was seeping out, literally dripping from the pads, like water from a supersaturated sponge.

The tiger's blood pressure drifted precipitously low from shock—so low that it was impossible for Kendall to locate a blood vessel that hadn't collapsed. After numerous attempts on multiple vessels, Kendall's competent hands finally managed to tap into the femoral artery on the inside of Meru's thigh. Once she hooked up the IV bag, starting the flow of antivenin, we almost immediately had the answers to all our questions. Within about 15 minutes lymph stopped dripping from the cat's footpads and the distension, starting at her shoulder, began to noticeably subside. Meanwhile, to mitigate the effects of shock we gently wrapped her limp body in a big thick blanket.

Ultimately, complete reduction in the swelling took more than just overnight, but by morning the tiger had obviously escaped any more serious damage or death. With all that extensively involved tissue, it was remarkable that the only permanent damage was a small amount of necrotic pad skin that sloughed off over the next few days.

Oh, and after a lengthy, thorough search of the exhibit, Dick never did find that rattlesnake.

One day I encountered a brazen zoo visitor posing for a picture, *sitting on top* of our biggest Galapagos tortoise.

The spatulate beak of a roseate spoonbill from a unique perspective.

Human Porcupine

The noble heritage of pronghorns, which are native only to North America, is frequently overlooked. These antelope have great stamina and are the second fastest land mammal (cheetahs being number one). They can reach speeds of up to 53 mph for a short burst, but with great endurance can run for many miles at half that speed. Even a 2-day old fawn can outrun a horse for a short distance. When alarmed, pronghorn puff out the white hair on their rumps as a dramatic signal to the others of the herd. In the fall breeding season, a male will gather females into a harem, which he jealously and very aggressively guards from rivals.

These antelope eat grass, sagebrush and other vegetation in the dry open lands of western North America. Before pioneers took over the prairies pronghorn once numbered well over 40-50 million, often roaming in association with staggering numbers of bison. Due to habitat encroachment and over-hunting, however, only about 600,000 wander the wild today. Sometimes to their detriment these animals are exceedingly curious, often approaching a predator. This is most likely to keep tabs on its whereabouts, which is actually a good survival strategy. Early settlers used this inquisitive trait to their advantage by waving a handkerchief on the end of a stick, enticing the naïve innocents into firing range.

The name "prong*horn*" is actually somewhat of a misnomer. Deer shed and re-grow their antlers, made of bone, annually. The true horns of cattle or bison are never shed and are made of keratin (a protein also found in hair, nails and hooves) growing on a bony core. The horn sheath of prong-horns is a little of both. Keratin grows over a bony extension of the skull, but is shed each year, and the spiky bone is exposed until the new sheath grows in. Both sexes sport the horns, but the females' are comparatively small. The horns of the males can be as much as 15 inches long. Also, true horns are not branched. The male pronghorns' sheaths are forked with the longer tine hooking at the tip. They use their horns for defense against predators and during spectacular sparring in battles with other males during breeding season.

Growing up around humans, orphaned hoofstock (such as deer) that have been hand-raised never learn to fear us. So once reaching adulthood, they can be perilous to work around, males in particular. Keepers may interact with them for years with no problem, becoming lulled into a false sense of safety. Then with hormones, territoriality, or some other inexplicable reason, one may decide to go after you. That was what happened to Janie and an American pronghorn antelope.

DICK HILTON

In the late 1800s pronghorn were senselessly slaughtered as well as bison, their once great numbers dropping precipitously.

The pronghorn enclosure, a large paddock located in the "desert habitat" section of the zoo, housed two parent-raised females and two hand-raised males. As the keeper delivered the grain at feeding time, the parent-raised animals typically kept a little distance from her, but the males stumbled over each other at the trough to be first to eat.

At the edge of the exhibit near the feeder grew a large patch of stunningly pretty Christmas cholla. This cactus produces gauzy yellow-bronze flowers, then bright red and juicy grape-sized fruits that last all winter long. The multi-branched plant grows wide and tall from its base. It is as wicked as it is attractive, for tangles of skinny, crisscrossing branches bear 2-inch-long spines as thin as needles and just as sharp. Miniscule barbs covering papery sheaths on the spines penetrate any cloth or flesh coming in contact with them. Admire its beauty all you want, but definitely don't touch!

Easy-going Janie had sensuous brown eyes and often wore her chestnut brown hair in a thick braided rope trailing down her back. She had worked this section of the zoo for many years, so she knew the animals as well as they knew her. Up until the incident, this particular pronghorn had never exhibited aggression. But as she filled the feeder this one morning, all of sudden one of the males lunged at Janie, butting her with his head. She reeled with surprise but thought that would be the end of it. Then he knocked the feed bucket out of her hands. Before she could react, with another quick butt he shoved the keeper off her feet. She slammed onto her back—right into the nasty cholla branches. Falling into that cactus was horrific enough, but then the maniacal 130-lb. pronghorn came after Janie again. Over and over again. His repeated butts punched the breath out of her; she couldn't even scream for help. Relentlessly he rammed her in the stomach, mashing her deeper into the penetrating spines.

Fortunately for Janie, this pronghorn had damaged his horns when they first started to grow in, so they splayed out abnormally wide to the sides. Otherwise the keeper would have been brutally eviscerated by those hooked tips. Still, she needed to somehow get out of the excruciating cactus and away from this bedeviled beast intent on assaulting her. With no other options, she grabbed hold of his throat and began to squeeze. At the last second she astutely thought to seize one of his horns with her other hand. When the pronghorn reared back to get away from the chokehold, he also pulled Janie up and out of the cactus, enabling her to finally slip away.

It was at this point that I got the emergency radio call, and now faced the unique dilemma of how to transport Janie to the nearby hospital. The entire back of her body from head to heel was riddled with the wicked cactus spines and she felt woozy. She refused an ambulance. Obviously she couldn't sit, or lie on her back, and didn't want to lie face down in the bed of the pickup truck. So with just minimal discomfort to add to what she had already greatly suffered, she opted to gingerly kneel on a cushion between the seats of the zoo's van as we sped off to the nearby emergency room. Poor Janie spent the rest of the day in the hospital while nurses plucked out the invasive spines and barbs. She then had to soak in a tub to coax out those that had broken off under her skin before they festered and caused infection.

Needless to say, now no keeper enters the exhibit without first locking *all* the pronghorns in the barn.

Runaway Ram

Working with wild animals in a zoo obviously exposes one to risks, but sometimes a hazard may present itself in an unlikely place. Many zoos often have a Children's Zoo with some sort of "contact area." These environments allow small children to safely mingle with and touch a variety of friendly barnyard or hand-raised animals.

The Children's Zoo attendant, Kurt, was a nimble 19-year-old with the slim build of youth. His brown hair, slippery and toothpick-straight, constantly needed to be pushed away from his eyes. He felt impatient to begin his animal keeper career but had to prove himself first. Most inexperienced keepers start out in the Children's Zoo where docile domestics pose less likelihood of any serious mishaps.

With arms folded and chin on his chest, Kurt leaned against a post in the contact yard one day, imagining the future when he would finally be a reptile keeper. Listless from the heat he sank deeper into the daydream. In his peripheral vision he perceived the play of long, exaggerated shadows cast by the late afternoon summer sun. It had been a slow and boring day, too hot for many visitors. All the goats and sheep sought patches of shade and sprawled about for a siesta. All but one that is. Drifting back to reality, Kurt brushed the hair from his eyes and flicked his tongue over his parched lips. He noticed the stretched shadow of a sheep that seemed to consistently mirror the movements of a man's shadow as he led his grandson around the paddock.

Sure enough, one of the frisky young sheep was stalking the back pocket of the kindly grandfather as he bent over to pick up his tot. The contact area was devoid of any greenery to nibble, so the bored goats and sheep typically shadowed zoo visitors, ever watchful for some edible diversion. They had a lengthy history of absconding with zoo brochures, glasses cases, Kleenex, checkbooks, or any other item poking out of a pocket or purse that they thought might be a tasty treat. And they learned to be quick about it or stingy humans would try to purloin the booty from them.

Hoping to go unnoticed, this scheming sheep plucked the colorful zoo map from the man's pocket and took off, hastily chomping on his treasure. Then—wouldn't you know it—that busybody attendant came in hot pursuit to spoil his triumph! A moment later though, making an abrupt and completely unexpected stop in mid-stride, the sheep became an unyielding barrier to the momentum of Kurt's oncoming body.

CINDY BARRY

"It was like I moved in slow motion," Kurt woefully exclaimed to the other keepers. "My legs thudded into the sheep and I went sailing over him like an Olympic gymnast vaulting over a pommel horse. The next thing I knew, my face was in the dirt and I had agonizing pain in my right arm."

Not only did Kurt suffer a fractured humerus, but also ceaseless humiliation. Though his arm healed months ago, fellow keepers still mercilessly remind Kurt of his mishap, warning him about working around those treacherous and conniving, "map-eating" sheep.

⎯⎯⎯➤

Other barnyard animals exhibited in the Children's Zoo lived in a small barn with three adjoining paddocks. The residents included a pair of handsome Nubian goats, a karakul sheep in the center pen, and a trio of pygmy goats. All the keepers dreaded working with the male pygmy goat as he had a persistent and disgusting habit of following just a footstep behind, then rudely planting his nose in your crotch as soon as you stopped moving. It didn't matter how many times you shooed him away, as soon as you turned back to your work, the perverted beast came sniffing about again. Worse yet, sometimes after a sniff he'd step back with his eyes staring blankly ahead and nose in the air, his lips twitching and tootsie roll tongue sticking out. We usually tried to get his pen raked before the zoo opened to avoid that repulsive show before an audience. Besides all that, the male reeked of a particularly pungent goat aroma that seemed to cling to your clothes just by looking at him. You couldn't escape the smell of him for the rest of the day, and of course worried that anyone who came close by might think your body was the source of that awful stink.

But the pygmy goats weren't really a menace—that disagreeable distinction went to the zoo's old karakul ram, "Krazy." The karakul, with its huge bulging tail of stored fat, is a Middle Eastern variety of sheep prized for its coat (unfortunately for the lambs the pelt quality peaks at only three days old). Krazy's massive horns ominously spiraled in big coils along the sides of his head. We housed him in the center pen, and to keep innocent little fingers from getting crushed, a few feet inside the guardrail from where the public stood we installed a second rail.

When it came time to rake the paddocks, we easily lured all the goats into their stalls with a reward of food. However, for sheer orneriness it seemed, the karakul refused to enter the barn. He'd just stand in the doorway, staring ahead with that unnerving blank gaze goats and sheep have that never makes eye contact. Krazy obsessed about always challenging anyone and anything with his horns.

Keepers even had to keep an eye on him when raking in the adjoining pens. Don't stand too close to the rail on his side when bending over to sweep the rakings into the shovel or he'll sneak up and deliver a severe butt to your butt and knock you to the ground. No way could a keeper step into the ram's pen to rake by himself. An annoying inconvenience, another keeper always had to leave his job to accompany the raking keeper, so we resorted to raking the ram's pen only every two or three days. Keepers still risked injury by directly sharing his space, until finally a keeper came up with a novel solution by clever use of the sheep's own behavior, as follows.

While I safely stood in the adjoining Nubian goats' pen, using my body as bait, Krazy readily shuffled over to the rails with his big ugly tail flapping against his legs. Once he started his butting routine we took advantage of his position and hastily affixed his horns to the rail by tying a long strap around them in a figure eight. This secured him for the quick few minutes it took to then run back around through the barn and safely service his paddock. (We might get an occasional complaint from a zoo visitor but easily explained our sensible strategy for dealing with this butt-happy beast.)

Every day we tied his horns to the rail, and every day he fell for the luring ruse. He never figured it out. In fact, he didn't seem to mind being constrained. This single-minded ram acted invigorated, as if he had encountered a particularly strong rival. Once the "challenger's horns" magically disentangled from Krazy, the "rival" seemed to have disappeared. He had obviously been intimidated by Krazy's strength and tenacity. The karakul ram would strut about with his nose in the air, proudly sniffing to see if he could tell in which direction the cowardly contender had snuck off to.

X-Rated Exhibition

An African gray parrot looks as handsome as it is smart. He dresses in pale gray plumage with a contrasting accent of crimson tail feathers. Many of the smaller gray feathers are tinged with a delicate line of white on the edges, creating an attractive scalloped appearance. There is an oddly unnatural look to the straw-colored iris. And the slate black beak contradicts the powdery white cheek patch of naked skin that feels as soft as kid leather. Grays are notorious for their precise mimicking ability. The zoo's education department had an old female gray whose previous owner suffered the constant lung congestion of emphysema. The bird was in perfect health but so impeccably mimicked the awful sound of the phlegmy cough she seemed surely on death's doorstep!

One particular gray, "Alex," of recent fame in Seattle, underwent extensive studies at various collegiate institutions to examine his ability to distinguish colors, names of items (like a key or block of wood), count up to six objects, and other unique communications. He proved himself to be a pretty sophisticated birdbrain!

The zoo exhibited a pair of grays that had been donated from someone about a year before. Apparently, neither had ever been trained to talk—we never heard them utter a word. Their demeanor was regal and silent. Standing at my cart one morning, I filled a food cup with seed mix, nuts, fruits and

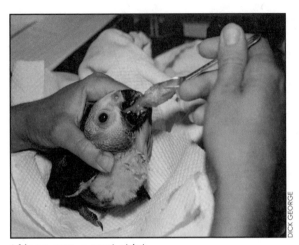

African gray parrot chick

vegetables to carry into the grays' exhibit. Meanwhile I fielded questions from an excited group of school children that gathered to watch my activity. I glanced up to note where the birds were perched before entering the exhibit and, uh oh. How come I see only one bird? The padlock is locked, and nothing seems amiss with the aviary. Then I realized that, for the first time, one of the parrots must be in the nest box that we had installed about a month before. Trying not to make any disturbing sounds or vibrations I entered the aviary and with great prudence stepped over to the box. Then I gingerly unlatched the inspection door to peek inside. What joy! The female looked at me looking at her as she stood straddling over a little white egg! At the very moment that I opened the inspection door, though, that sweet surprise turned sickeningly sour.

The male, fretful and anxious while observing all this, became sorely agitated by my approach to their nest. He stiffly swaggered up and down the long horizontal perch at the front of the exhibit where the large crowd of attentive children stood. With a maniacal, menacing stare the pupils of his eyes repeatedly zoomed large then small and back again. This bird that had always been silent now screamed, endlessly repeating a string of profanities with exceptional clarity: "God damn bird, shit, God damn bird, shit, God damn bird, shit…"

The cursing continued non-stop in front of all those intently listening, innocent ears. So in absolute compliance I gently but quickly closed up the nest box and made a hasty exit. With the threat of my presence gone, the parrot calmed down and thankfully quit his offensive language.

This first nesting failed to produce fertile eggs, but a year later two of three eggs hatched and the precious chicks fledged successfully. We assume that the youngsters never learned to cuss from their parents for ever since that memorable incident we avoided going anywhere near the grays' nest box, especially when any zoo visitors stood in earshot.

Olive baboons have specialized cheek pouches for storing food as they forage.

What's in the Bag?

T his job is so boring," Becky whined to her coworker, Jen. They dragged another bulging, heavy garbage bag from the trashcan and knotted it. Then they tossed it in the back of the golf cart with the other accumulated bags.

Jen replied, "Yeah, but at least we get to drive around outdoors, and see all the animals every day. We could be stuck indoors, cleaning a big office building." She snapped open a new bag, stuffed it in the can, and replaced the lid. That finished the cans at the zoo entrance. A 20-foot-high bridge spanned the lake here, bringing zoo visitors from the parking lot to the ticket booths at the entrance.

The next stop was the string of cans in the Children's Zoo section of the zoo. To get there, Jen and Becky hopped back on the golf cart and sped off on the zoo's perimeter service road that followed the lake shoreline. The road cut into the hillside high above the lake, and as they drove along Jen peered down at a big white trash bag floating in the middle of the murky lake. It looked all ballooned open and had drifted some distance from both the bridge and road.

"Looks like we're going for a boat ride this afternoon," Jen said. "Let's load up the rowboat from the Children's Zoo lake after we finish the cans there. We can skirt the shorelines and pick up floating litter as long as we're out there. It's been a while since we patrolled this lake for garbage. And if we go out later when it's really hot being on the water will feel refreshing."

Later that afternoon, the girls paddled out to retrieve the bag. As they neared it, however, Becky noticed that now it didn't quite look like a plastic bag. Floating closer, she could see that it was white fabric. Closer still, and it became obvious that it was actually a man's shirt, a pretty big one at that. Ooh, and what's this? The man is STILL WEARING IT!

Jen frantically paddled the boat to shore, while Becky screeched into the radio for a security guard to meet them at the launch ramp. Scooping up an occasional dead duck or yucky fish carcass amongst other floating debris could sometimes be part of their various janitorial duties, but this was downright gruesome. Suddenly the job wasn't so boring anymore.

The coroner determined drowning as the probable cause of death, and that the man probably had been in the cold lake water for 30 to 40 hours. Two nights before being discovered, while standing on the middle of the bridge he apparently went over the railing and sank. After bloating from the start of decomposition, his big body floated up and drifted far enough away from the bridge that visitors crossing into the zoo couldn't tell what the white spectacle might have been.

Who was he? Was it suicide? Murder? Or just a freak accident? The evidence the police gathered was sketchy at best. The victim had no wallet

A few of the multitude of the lake's turtles take advantage of a submerged log to warm up in the sun.

and there was nothing distinctive about his clothes, just an XXL plain white shirt, black slacks, and tennis shoes. No abandoned car waited in vain in the parking lot, and no witness reported any unusual activity. Unfortunately his body lay face down in the water and the lake teemed with ravenous turtles and fish, so creating a sketch to help discern his identity was out of the question. Any fingerprints had been nibbled away too.

Unless a witness (or guilt-ridden perpetrator) comes forward we will never know the man's identity or exactly what happened to him. The most intriguing clue of the event also remains unsolved: The mystery of why the pants were down on this anonymous dead man in the lake, clinging to his ankles.

At the expense of elongated legs, vertebrae, skull, heart, and tongue, an adult male giraffe's body is necessarily short in proportion.

Unlike lions and tigers, cheetahs have a more skittish temperament and can be difficult to breed in a zoo setting.

On Call

We didn't have 24-hour security at one small zoo where I worked, so the staff took turns to be on call after hours to deal with any rare emergency that might arise. At around 1:30 AM one night when it was my turn, the police department telephoned to alert me that one of the motion sensor alarms had been triggered. The zoo's free-roaming peacocks flying up to or down from a building roof instigated occasional false alarms, but we always investigated just in case.

When I arrived this time, the police already had two guys in their late teens in handcuffs. They looked pretty forlorn as they sprawled on the bench across from Zippy the chimpanzee's exhibit. As usual, alcohol was involved, and who knows what these two yahoos had been up to. I made a quick check of the chimp and his exhibit and other nearby ones and all seemed perfectly fine. But Zippy ran around hooting non-stop, and I couldn't be sure if he was more scared, excited, or enthralled with all the late night hubbub. The officers loaded the two perpetrators into the squad car and headed for the precinct jail. Meanwhile I trundled over to the office to record what had happened and to reset the alarm. As I locked up the office I glanced at my watch and was pleased to see that I could still catch a few more hours of sleep before returning for work at 7:00.

A typical 6-foot-high wrought iron fence of vertical bars topped with decorative little "spears" enclosed the perimeter of the zoo. There was a horizontal bar running across the bottom a foot above the ground and another a foot below the top. There were occasional gaps in the plantings, but for most of its distance lush landscaping of tall bushes planted on the outside obscured the fence. My path from the office to the perimeter gate in the fence was only dimly lit by a streetlight in the zoo's parking lot.

Zoos can be spooky places at night, particularly when you're there all alone, but I tried not to let my imagination run wild which wasn't easy. Out of necessity, living by myself as a single woman for the past fifteen years made me hypersensitive to perceived dangers, real or imagined. So I was scurrying down the trail when, in my peripheral vision, I just happened to notice what appeared to be the tips of a pair of sneakers protruding through the fence, standing on the lower horizontal bar. I stopped dead in my tracks hoping my eyes would quickly adjust, but it still took a moment for what I could see to register—there were feet in those shoes, and legs attached to those feet! Leafy branches and darkness obscured the rest of him. Standing in the open by myself, the streetlight suddenly seemed to glare down at me and become my own personal bright spotlight, making me feel especially conspicuous. I envisioned this third culprit taking revenge on me after witnessing his partners in crime hauled away in the squad car. I couldn't have been more frightened as morbid scenarios played through my head and I frantically tried to think of what might be my best chance to get out of this terrifying situation.

Like replaying a movie scene, I can still see myself with hair flying wildly behind my head while I ran, escaping down the path to the gate and cramming the key into the padlock. As I fled for my life I left the gate wide open, jumped into my car and gunned it to a nearby convenience market just around the corner that thankfully had a pay phone out front (obviously this is way before the advent of cell phones!).

Just as I was dialing for help another cop happened to come cruising by. Ah, serendipity! He noticed my car parked facing the wrong direction on the street with the door hanging open, and me gesturing wildly while on the phone. After a frantic recounting of events, he returned to the zoo with me and cautiously approached the fence where I had perceived the suspect.

Well now that's kind of weird. After all this time, here were the toes of the shoes in the exact same place, still sticking through the bars. When the officer scanned his flashlight up the suspect's body we saw his arms draped over the top horizontal bar and his face lodged between the vertical bars. Apparently too drunk to navigate climbing over the fence with his cohorts, this guy had passed out strung up on the fence with the additional support of the thick bushes behind him.

Hurrah! Another one hauled off to the local jail to sober up and face a few legal charges. What I really appreciated though was this officer waiting for me to re-set the alarm and lock up again, and kindly lingering until I drove away. By the time I finished the short drive home my leg muscles throbbed from constant quivering and my fingers ached from the death grip I had on the steering wheel. It was still only about 3 AM but there was certainly no going back to sleep after all that night's drama.

These young and playful hand-raised toucan chicks liked to poke, pull, and shake anything in reach of their ever-lengthening beaks.

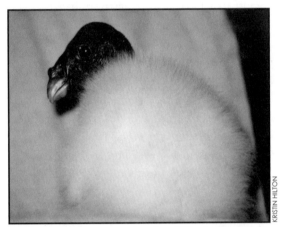

KRISTIN HILTON

How can such an endearing little fuzzball with his penetrating blue eyes grow up to have such revolting eating habits?

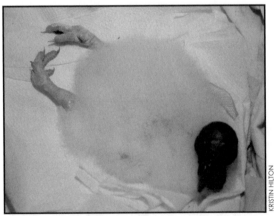

KRISTIN HILTON

I finally managed to catch a picture of the king vulture chick's most unusual sleeping position before he stood up.

Just Between You and Me

At Happy Hour at a local bar one evening Rich told some fellow barstool buddies about one of his more memorable incidents as a keeper, a favorite subject of conversation among the beer drinkers. "I came in for evening keeper duty one time," Rich said, nibbling on some peanuts, "but I was way early. So I just cruised around on the cart a little, waiting for all the keepers to meet up at the main office at the end of the day, to write up their reports." He went on to explain to nearby bar patrons that the Daily Report is where a keeper records everything significant that happened in his work area that day, including births, deaths, transfers, health concerns, maintenance issues, etc.

"After my drive, though, there still weren't any keepers at the office. So I decided to wait around at the orangutan exhibit where my roommate, Kyle, worked. I've told you about 'Bo,' the big male orangutan, well, he's one of my favorite animals to be around.

"As I walked toward Bo's room to offer him some grapes, I looked in and, whoa, what's all this? I saw these shreds of light blue fabric everywhere. Back then, the keeper uniform," Rich noted, "was jeans and a blue chambray work shirt. I took a closer look and sure enough, it was someone's shirt all torn to bits. And I thought, oh, man—this orang is the one that bit off my fingernail a few months ago. Damn, he has to have gotten somebody, and maybe that's why none of the keepers are around.

"I jumped on the cart and drove back to the office, where Kyle, Ben and a few other keepers were standing around, just kinda casually chatting. It was winter, so everybody had jackets on, and I could see the collars of everyone's blue shirts sticking out from underneath. I walked up to Kyle and pulled him aside.

"I quickly scanned around again to look at the other keepers' clothes and I whispered to him, 'Kyle, Bo got hold of somebody—there's a keeper's shirt in his room all torn up.'

"And Kyle leaned in closer next to my ear and said, 'I know. Don't tell anybody, don't breathe a word.'

"He turned towards me, away from everybody, and unzipped his jacket. When he opened it up, I could see that all he had on was the collar and top two buttons of that shirt. The rest of his chest was bare! Kyle zipped his jacket back up and we just stood there, not saying anything, for the rest of the ten minutes or so until all the keepers left and I resumed my routine. Neither of us said a word, and everybody just went on home. Kyle never explained what happened that day, and I didn't have the heart to ask."

Wild Sex

An oasis in the desert, migrating waterfowl flock to the zoo's string of revitalizing lakes as a welcome stopover during their long journeys. Hunger and exhaustion suppress their urge to flee from the throngs of zoo visitors wandering the shoreline trails. The feathered visitors include pintail, mallard, widgeon, and shoveler ducks, and the more diminutive ring-necked and ruddy ducks, and cinnamon and green-winged teal. Many over-winter at the zoo (true "snowbirds"), and a few that are somehow not up to the rigorous return journey stay longer. Some never leave—most notoriously the ubiquitous mallard, which seems to have no hesitation in putting up with humans in exchange for a soft life. It was always a grand spectacle to see the crowded masses of waterfowl covering the surfaces of the lakes. What a heartbreak to witness their diminished numbers just in my lifetime.

One sultry day in late spring, long after the hordes of migrators had left, I worked at a parrot exhibit next to one of the lakes when I heard a commotion of splashing water and raucous quacking of ducks. I saw a single wild mallard hen being mercilessly mobbed by eleven males. This poor duck was the only female in sight, so the males fought each other ruthlessly for a turn at breeding her. Each stood on her back grabbing the feathers of her neck with his bill as she desperately tried to paddle to shore. Three and four at a time jostled for position, over and over again and constantly displacing one another. Utterly exhausted by all this frenzy, she dragged herself on shore, only to be swarmed anew once the drakes had easier footing. The hen plunged back to the relative refuge of the water, but there she risked drowning. The obsessed males kept shoving her head under water as they grasped at her neck for stability. She became so weak that she barely kept her head up anymore, gasping for air whenever she could. The poor little thing was probably a young bird and was just so overwhelmed by the unrelenting gang rape that she didn't know what to do.

I decided I just had to intervene, and the next time she stumbled ashore I dashed in amongst the tumult and scooped her up in my arms. Running to my cart I sat with her on my lap for a few minutes while I decided what to do next. Her neck had been ripped bare of feathers, and the skin raw and bloody from the rough treatment by the males. I sped off to the lake at the Children's Zoo where to my relief there wasn't another duck in sight. Squatting down at the water's edge I gently released her and she took off flying to get away from this new terror of being handled by a human. The pathetic bird was still pretty exhausted so just skimmed the surface of the water, but made it to the center of the big lake.

I felt so relieved to see her finally free from the harassment of all those aggressors. But then immediately felt a wave of dismay ripple through my stomach. What the heck? Where did all these drakes magically appear from? They flew to the hen from all directions. The lake had seemed devoid of ducks, but apparently they had been napping on the shore out of sight, seeking relief from the heat. So this ambush of fresh and rested males mobbed the little hen, even more relentlessly than the others. There must have been twenty of them impatiently waiting their turns.

Dejected beyond words, I stood helplessly watching as the horror of it all sank in. Finally I couldn't stand it any more and turned away. Perhaps she could have endured the activity at that first lake if I hadn't intervened, perhaps not. And now at this lake she was too far from shore to drag herself out of the water, and probably still too exhausted to fly anymore. I didn't see how she could survive this new onslaught, but could think of nothing I could do to help. I'd have to drive to the back of the zoo for a couple of big nets and find someone to help me. Then go to the dock at the other lake to retrieve the boat and load it up. We'd drive to the Children's Zoo lake, unload the boat, and then paddle out to the hen. This would have taken way too much time to be able to rescue her.

In case she had died, I searched over the next couple of days but never found her body floating along the lakeshore, so perhaps with the brief respite on my lap she was able to summon the strength to fly off the water and find some thick bushes to hide in. I will always wonder what her ultimate fate was, and have felt as guilty as if I had drowned her myself. I was new on the job and didn't know any better. In retrospect I should have just put her in a box for a few hours to recover, then released her back to her lake at dusk. The hard lesson from this was that sometimes it is best just to leave nature alone.

The mallard is the ancestor of all domestic duck breeds except the muscovy duck. Males sport that distinctive curl of feathers above the tail, making it easy to sex all-white ducks like the Pekin variety.

The ostrich is the largest of all birds and incredibly supports its 300 lbs. on only two toes; all other birds have three or four toes.

Yoyo Mama

Contrary to what one might think, instances of mischief or vandalism occur somewhat less often on busy days at the zoo. Perhaps that's because there would be more potential witnesses to a perpetrator's feeding, rock throwing, or other more serious misbehaviors.

One gloomy day when hardly any visitors roamed the zoo grounds, I happened to notice something odd about the female ostrich as I drove by the display. She acted fine, but a peculiar lump swelled the base of her long neck. The shape of the bulge suggested that she had swallowed a yoyo that a visitor must have thrown into the exhibit. For some reason the big flightless birds collectively known as ratites (ostriches, emus, cassowaries, and rheas) always seem attracted to shiny metal or brightly colored objects. Which perhaps is not as unusual as it might seem. To an ostrich's eye, the bright gleam off a dewy yellow flower petal may indicate an enticing food morsel. So they will persistently peck at the sparkling clip that secures the ring of keys to a keeper's belt loop. To avoid having them accidentally disappear down an obsessive bird's long gullet we try to remember to slip the dangling keys out of sight into a pocket anytime we work around these fixated birds.

After reporting the odd neck protuberance to the veterinarian he decided that we needed to check it out, and within a half hour a crew of keepers convened at the ostrich pen. Wielding two large panels of plywood with handles affixed

CINDY BARRY

to them we maneuvered her one slow step at a time until she was crammed into a corner of the paddock. This made her unable to move and the plywood shield protected us from her dangerous legs. At 250 to 300 lbs., an ostrich's powerful, meaty drumsticks can deliver a kick mighty enough to kill a lion.

As the vet gently manipulated the round mass the protracted journey up her long, sinuous neck I shoved my shoe tips into the chain link fence to be eye-to-eye with this 6-foot-tall bird. Once the lump had been coaxed to the top of her throat, I became the lucky designee with the distasteful task of sticking my hand into her gaping mouth. Out popped not a yoyo, but something else disgustingly slimy and wet. She had somehow swallowed whole a glistening red apple that a zoo visitor tossed into her exhibit. It may not have been a toy that blocked her throat, but it seemed fitting that Yoyo become her new name anyway.

How Does He Know?

To their dismay, many parrot owners may discover that their pet prefers one sex to another in their human companions.

"Pecos," the zoo's blue-fronted Amazon parrot, was a particularly aggressive bird who wouldn't tolerate any cagemates. He absolutely hated female keepers and wouldn't allow them anywhere near his exhibit. He delighted in the company of male keepers, and ignored all the women that visited the zoo. But if a female keeper ventured near the door, Pecos put on a big show of squawking, mock attacks, and riotous laughter. The keeper could be viciously assaulted if she unwisely ignored his tantrums and entered the exhibit. Seeing the pupils of his eyes repeatedly zooming micro to macro during these wild fits felt especially unnerving, like finding yourself in a scene from the exorcist.

One time, Snoozie and I tried to see if we couldn't outsmart him. (Suzie earned that nickname when she claimed that her "favorite time of day is night, when I know I'll be going to bed.") She worked in a different section of the zoo and so Pecos had never seen her before. Snoozie dressed up in gloves, sunglasses, and an oversized, bulky uniform jacket. To help look more masculine she tucked her long hair up into a baseball cap. She was careful not to say anything. But all of that didn't fool him. It's a good thing Snoozie had all that clothing on because he was quiet at first, but the mo-

CINDY BARRY

ment she stepped through the aviary doorway the parrot flew at her in a rage. First he landed on top of her head, and then attacked her shoulder when she instinctively crouched over to protect her face. Pecos repeatedly thrashed her with powerful wing beats while fiercely clawing Snoozie with his sharp toe- nails and biting holes in her jacket. It took no more than those few terrifying seconds before she wisely put an abrupt end to our little experiment.

Sexual dimorphism is the term for the difference in appearance (such as coloration, size, antlers, etc.) between adult males and females of the same species. This is obvious in mammals like deer and African lion, and birds such as mallard, pheasant, and ostrich. But males and females of many other species, like Amazon parrots, often look identical. Unless an Amazon lays an egg the only way to tell the sex for sure is to look directly at the internal go- nads with a laparoscope, a fine surgical instrument with a lighted optical tube. One day, a visiting veterinarian who perfected the surgical sexing technique offered to help us figure out our "unknowns." We were astonished to find that our ornery parrot Pecos, who we always assumed to be male, was actually a female. How is it that parrots can discern between human sexes when we can't tell what sex they are? How does *she* know?

What a miserable bunch of aviaries for a keeper to face every day. Dotting the zoo's lakeshore in little clusters sat thirteen exhibits housing various species of parrots. A generous retired bird enthusiast kindly donated his old cages when the struggling zoo came into creation. They provided comparatively generous space (each measured 5 feet wide, 8 feet long, and 7 feet high) for exhibiting one or two birds, and gave the keeper room to move around when working inside. So that was all nice. The problem was the door situation. A second door with a small vestibule attached to an exhibit (we called a "keeper safety") virtually eliminates the risk of an animal accidentally getting out while the keeper services the cage. Not one of these cages had that setup.

Having no safety wasn't always a risk for most of the birds, but individuals with aggressive or flighty temperament demanded extreme caution. The keepers always groaned when servicing these aviaries because whoever designed them made the mesh door a meager 20 inches wide and only 3 feet high to limit the risk of escape; he had to have been either a child, a midget or a sadist. Here's why. While laden with a bowl of fresh food, scrub brush, hand rake, and dustpan, the keeper had to squat down then twist sideways to quickly squeeze through the doorway, landing on a knee. He had to be a lithe contortionist to slither in there, especially on a cold, rainy winter day with hat, boots and bulky jacket on. Then he had to drop everything from his hands so that he could jump up while pulling the door shut and latch it behind him. To add to the exasperation, some of those exhibits had no hose bib nearby, so he had to tote fresh drinking water in a bucket every day.

Most of the birds housed in these aviaries cooperated by perching quietly on a high branch at the far end of the cage when a keeper entered, but not "Chica" and "Dingdong." These two yellow-naped Amazon parrots (former unwanted pets of course) weren't particular to one sex or another; they acted hostile to all of the keepers. It didn't matter who it was. As soon as they saw you coming they exhibited raucous, aggressive behavior, and always targeted your face if you got close. Every day we outsmarted them by luring the parrots to the side of the aviary that the door opened into. Then we would briefly poke our fingers in the mesh as bait to get them to come down toward the ground. By quickly swinging the door all the way open they were then effectively trapped in the corner between the door and side of the cage (until they climbed up to the top of that ridiculous faux barrier of course). Once they were somewhat cornered behind the door we could make a mad grab for the food and water dishes, then slam the door shut. To return the cleaned and refilled bowls we simply repeated the deceptive maneuver. Chica and Dingdong, so preoccupied with showing off their rage, never figured out our tactics and fell for the ruse every time. But the real challenge came about twice a week when the aviary needed raking. The chore took two jittery keepers in a great show of trust and teamwork, one frantically raking while the other held a trash can lid as a shield to protect our faces from the birds' frenzied attacks.

It's hard to imagine why no one wanted the endearing Chica and Dingdong as pets in their home, isn't it?

Apparently someone thought that those thirteen aviaries didn't present enough of a challenge for keepers, so there were five other aviaries located here and there around the zoo with that same stupid miniature door design and no keeper safety. These were bigger cages, giant cubes measuring 8 feet by 8 feet by 8 feet. But this was the kicker—try to picture all this—each cage had been *elevated* 2 feet high on a 3-foot-square concrete pedestal that protruded into the bottom. The floor of the cage consisted of a 2 ½-foot wide perimeter of ½- by 1-inch mesh surrounding that pedestal. The rimmed top of the pedestal was filled with dirt (yes, I'm calling it dirt—it was too dry and lifeless to be called soil). The big selling point of this design was that the seed hulls and fecal matter could conveniently drop through the mesh floor to the ground below.

So once the keeper opened the short, narrow door, mindful not to let any birds out, the challenge here was to hop up the 2 feet to the threshold of the doorway, meanwhile squeezing sideways and hunched over. And all this while juggling the usual array of food dish, scrub brush, and hand rake (that big square of dirt still needed raking). Once inside, then she had to balance precariously on the 3-inch-wide support straps of metal in the corners that connected the cage to the pedestal (holding the structure up above the ground). Without hesitation in the momentum, while balancing on one foot she kicked the door shut with her other, hoping to land on a support to regain her balance. These cages were old and the mesh of the floor had stressed over the years. If she accidentally put all her weight on it she risked having her foot plunge through when the aging, rusted mesh might break free of the frame. She had to work in there ever mindful of balancing on the supports. Then, with arms loaded again, she had to jump out and down while twisting to exit the cage, while watchful of the birds' whereabouts.

Being messy and frequently picky eaters, a great portion of the parrots' uneaten seeds wastefully ended up lying under the cage with no way for the intended birds to access them. This debris invited unwelcome interlopers such as pigeons, house sparrows and rodents to scavenge. To soften the look of the pedestal and metal frame landscapers had planted lush, colorful shrubbery. Very attractive, but now the final merits of the elevated aviary were revealed when the keeper had to virtually stand on her head to reach into the narrow 2 feet of space between cage bottom and ground and rake up all that waste from in between the bushes that surrounded the elevated cage. I'm exhausted just reliving the fond memories.

On a visit back to the zoo some years after I had left I noticed that the pedestals of all those cages were gone, and the aviaries sat sensibly on the ground. All were handsomely landscaped. Not only that, the keepers now used full size doors and safety vestibules at each. But I'll bet those keepers aren't as fit and trim as we were. I hope they appreciate the sacrifices of their previous coworkers that finally yielded all these logical conveniences.

———

"What kind of animal are you, ha ha?!" As if those miserable cages weren't enough to deal with. A keeper working in an exhibit has to endure this question pretty frequently. But we have to be nice, humor zoo visitors, let them think they're clever in coming up with some original witticism. Sure, this is the first time we've ever been asked that....

If we had a nickel for every time we heard that question we would all be rich.

DICK GEORGE

Some legendary keepers become giants among their peers.

Gogo
and the Garlicky Greek

The first thing every morning before beginning their work routine, keepers make a quick and cursory visual check of each exhibit under their care to be sure all is well. After six months working in the Children's Zoo, I had just transferred into this new section of the zoo that consisted of all different kinds of birds, and I couldn't be more excited. Snoozie, the keeper training me, said that I would probably rarely see "Gogo" in the exhibit with the other double yellow-headed parrot. I was curious to know why but she said just wait til later when we come back to feed them. As we drove past her aviary she yelled out "Gogo!" The parrot immediately responded in kind from deep inside the nest box, so we figured all was well with her. Parrots do pretty well mimicking most human words, but perhaps due to "inflexible lips" that wouldn't allow the "O" sound, her comical rendition of her name sounded more like "GwaGwa."

Robust, colorful, intelligent, long-lived, and very personable, this variety of Amazon parrot makes a popular (but in my view inappropriate) exotic pet. Snoozie told me that Gogo and her mate "Diego" accompanied their previous owner, a long-haul truck driver, back and forth across the country for many years. The trucker ultimately donated the pair of cabmates to the zoo. Diego, it seemed, was so amorous toward Gogo (or more likely neurotic from the stressful traveling lifestyle) that he preened the feathers on

Gogo's body to the extreme. She joined in too, and between the two of them the follicles that produced her once lustrous plumage became irreversibly damaged. The parrots mutilated the feathers to the point where, over time, they grew back thinner and weaker until finally they just didn't grow back at all. Any remaining abnormal pinfeathers seemed to annoy Gogo, so she ruthlessly plucked them out.

I couldn't believe what I saw the first time I peeked in the nest box. She looked ridiculous. Her head and wings bore most of the normal stunning yellow and green plumage (probably because she couldn't reach those). The flight feathers with their large quills probably hurt too much to pull out. The rest of poor Gogo looked like a pitiful plucked chicken. Her back, belly and legs were completely naked. This tropical bird suffered miserably at the zoo once the weather began to turn cold. She spent all her time snuggled in the nest box, briefly venturing out only for food and water.

The next day when I looked in the box to see how she was doing I took a closer look and was horrified when I noticed something else about her. This pathetic creature had such dry skin that it was peeling off in multiple layers of big sheets. It looked so extreme it didn't seem possible. I expressed my concerns to the curator, who promptly suggested that because winter was coming soon, wouldn't I want to take her to my house for the season? Without hesitation I agreed and she came home with me that very afternoon.

At the end of that first winter the curator further suggested not to bother to bring Gogo back, and for the next eight years until her death we remained devoted to each other. Handsome but abusive old Diego, still in his glorious plumage, remained at the zoo with some other cagemates we matched him up with. Ones that wouldn't allow him to pluck their feathers out.

While she lived with me, to keep Gogo warm, I modified a fluffy green sport sock by cutting slots for her legs and a hole for her to defecate through, and sewed on two ribbons to secure it like a bib. The sock couldn't fit more perfectly. I modified another pair of socks to always have clean "pseudo-feather suits" available, this time in golden yellow. I didn't plan it that way, but the green and gold socks ironically matched the feathers on her head and wings. I'm not sure that she ever showed a color preference, but perhaps Gogo felt more special than any other bird could in having day-to-day varying hues of "plumage."

A couple of times a week I would slather soothing lotion on her plump bare body to alleviate the incessant discomfort of her itchy dry skin. It no longer peeled off in layers like Phyllo pastry dough. She seemed to appreciate the relief from that and could often be seen gently preening her fuzzy attire.

She especially delighted in the "warming box" I set up for her. I couldn't have tolerated my house to be as hot as she would have preferred, even with her wearing that fluffy sock. So I scrounged a perfect discard from the zoo gift shop, a 16-inch-square metal display box 5 inches deep with a light socket inside. I installed wire mesh on the open side to keep her from having direct access to the heat-radiating bulb. The metal box had to stand on the floor because she couldn't fly more than a foot off the ground and only for a short distance at that. I rigged up a perch in a cardboard box tipped on end, setting the open side at an angle next to the bulb box. That way she could decide just how close she needed to be to the heat source. A towel draped over the two boxes held in the warmth, creating a cozy, bird-sized room.

An Amazon parrot's long toes are built for grasping branches, not walking flat on the ground. Gogo had to slide her feet stiffly across the floor to get around, and it took great effort for observers not to snicker at her ridiculously bowed legs. She shuffled along like one of those silly incline toys. To alleviate boredom I set up perches in various other locations on the floor, like in front of the sliding glass door so she could see outside. Gradually my house morphed into hers, but she rarely left that heated roost. It was the ideal setup for this poor bird who had suffered so much.

When Gogo first moved in with me I shared a house with two other girls to save on living expenses. They thought the parrot was great and delighted in getting her to whistle the boatswain's tune she loved to sing. Months later when one of the girls had to move out we were lucky to quickly find a new roommate, Ted, a college student. But things didn't work out so well right from the start. Maybe because of the garlic.

Ted was Greek, and he cooked everything with garlic. Lots of garlic. In fact, extreme excesses of garlic. The house stunk of it. His body sweated garlic. Our cleanliness standards certainly didn't match either. Whenever I had to pass by his reeking bedroom I held my breath and rushed down the hall because the door was always open and he never made his bed. By the look of them, those exposed, dingy gray sheets were never washed. They perpetually emanated the disgusting stink of stale garlic. I couldn't wait to move out on my own.

Apparently Gogo couldn't wait either. She singled Ted out mercilessly. But it wasn't the garlic in her case (or at least I don't think so). Typical of some parrots that prefer one sex of human to another she just never tolerated males. Her favorite time of attack was after Ted took a shower and would be padding down the hallway in his bare feet. This was one time she didn't mind leaving the warmth of her bulb box set-up. Patiently lying in wait outside the closed bathroom door, an incensed Gogo went into action once Ted emerged. Squawking the entire time, she flapped her wings furiously while shuffle-trotting after him as he dashed down the hall. She would savagely bite at Ted's ankles before he made it to the sanctuary of his bedroom, where he kicked his feet to separate them from this raging maniac.

It wasn't long after Ted moved in that Gogo and I moved out, much to everyone's relief.

In case you weren't aware, the only birds whose bodies are completely covered in feathers are penguins and a small handful of other types of birds. For all the rest, the feathers grow in narrow, well-defined tracts on their bodies known as pterilae (pronounced TAIR-ih-lay). Areas of bare skin without any tracts are referred to as apteria ("a" in Latin meaning "without"). Look for the "goose-bumps" evidence of pterilae the next time there's a plucked chicken or turkey about to be cooked in your kitchen.

The feathers in the symmetrical tracts spread out, giving the illusion of complete coverage over the bird's body. The varying, distinct patterns of pterilae sometimes help discern which families of birds may be evolutionarily related to each other. Poor Gogo really did look like a plucked chicken (and a greased one at that after the lotion was applied), and evidence of her tortured pterilae didn't even exist any more.

A Murder of Crows

With any luck you may have seen ravens frolic in aerobatic maneuvers, chase each other in dramatic "dog fights," or interlock feet while tumbling mid-flight. Their willful playfulness suggests more intellect than the average bird, also evidenced in experiments attempting to measure animal IQ separate from instinctual behaviors (for more information read Bernd Heinrich's fascinating books regarding behavior of the family of corvids: ravens, crows, magpies, jays and nutcrackers).

One day while on a vacation trip I sat eating lunch at the edge of Lake Powell and was treated to a most memorable show. A raucous raven wheeled around overhead for several passes then abruptly landed in a distant cluster of scrawny willow trees. The chunky bird landed on the tallest, most spindly of the trees with a self-aggrandizing air of "Well, here I am!" The branch yielded gracefully to the weight of the bird, bending down 8 feet or so. The raven loosened his grip on the perch and his body flipped so that he dangled upside down. He hung there for a moment then flapped furiously, pulling himself and the branch down another 3 or 4 feet. At this maximum point of the tree's flex the raven suddenly drew his wings against his body, catapulting himself and the branch almost as far to the opposite side and then swinging back to vertical. A living pendulum, he repeated the extreme performance numerous times, using the supple willow as his personal swing set.

Years later I found myself on a temporary 4-month leave of absence from my zookeeper job, working with another of the fascinating corvid family, the Hawaiian crow (locally known as "alala"). The entire population at the time was estimated to be around forty birds; there were six at the captive breeding facility on the Big Island where I worked. When the breeding pair first went to nest my job was to pull and artificially incubate the eggs. Then I would hand raise the hatchlings while the parents laid a second clutch of eggs that they would incubate and raise (a strategy known as "double clutching"). What an incredible opportunity to be part of this noble effort for these critically endangered birds.

The pair of crows diligently built their bulky nest of twigs and lined it with soft grasses to cushion the eggs, but no egg appeared. No matter what we tried, days, then weeks went by with not one egg (we had a camera trained on the nest so I could observe their activities from inside my cabin without disturbing them). So to pass the time I focused on fixing up the various enclosures of other endangered species and doing chores around the facility. I also enjoyed (an understatement!) my first helicopter ride, accompanying a fish and wildlife agent conducting a feral sheep survey around the slopes of 13,700' high Mauna Kea, Hawaii's highest peak (and my fabulous "back yard!")

Then one night shortly before my 4-month stint was up, my sound sleep was interrupted around 3 or 4 AM. In a confused state of total grogginess I noticed my cot violently jiggling, then skipping across the floor. It finally came to a stop in the middle of the room. Was this place haunted or what? It turned out to be the earthquake that introduced Kilauea's reawakening. The volcano's indescribable "curtain of fire" eruption made for even more impressive photos during a night visit. Ugh, what a dope. In all the excitement I loaded my camera with the previously exposed roll of film....

But, back to the facility and my extraordinary charges. Getting to know each of the ten individual crows at the facility became a daily delight. One of the previous year's babies, named "Lolo," stole my heart with his antics. Every day when I delivered the food tray he'd match my every step, hopping alongside my shoe. If I quickened the pace he used his wings to propel himself to catch up. When I abruptly stopped, he would throw himself on his back and wildly box the air with his feet. If I stood on my left leg and held my right foot just above him, he would grab the bottom of my shoe with his claws. He hung on as I repeatedly raised and lowered him—such a fun game for him that it was difficult to get him to let go when I tired of standing on one leg.

Other times he threw himself down on his side and pulled on my pants hem. He would tug at my sock, or peek up the pant leg while pecking my ankle (sometimes not so gently), or jam his probing beak between shoe and sock. Crows are known for their habit of caching food, so I guess I should consider myself lucky that he didn't try to stuff a chunk of hard-boiled egg in there.

In utter disappointment it became obvious to all of us working on the project that there would be no new additions that year to the dwindling population of these precious crows. *"Precious"* you might ask? How can a crow be considered anything but a pest? While similar in appearance and behavior to mainland crows, Hawaiian crows are a little smaller and more brownish. And they can't be found anywhere but on the Big Island. As with many other endemic species of Hawaiian birds their numbers are so perilously low

The bright scarlet red color inside the begging Hawaiian crow chick's mouth catches the attention of a parent crow with a food morsel.

that their population may not recover, even with heroic efforts by multiple local, state and federal agencies. As of 2010, no alala exist in the wild, and a mere 77 are housed at two captive breeding facilities on the Big Island and Maui. (By the way, like "a flock of geese" or "a pride of lions," a group of crows is referred to as "a murder.")

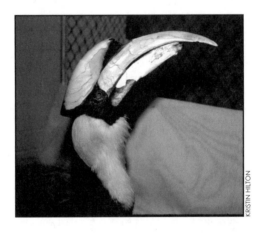

Zoo veterinarians sometimes encounter particularly unique challenges like this great hornbill's broken mandible.

Bo Remodels

Of all the keepers, Zeke probably let more animals out than anyone else: a roadrunner, the male leopard, a kangaroo, a zebra, and one of the oryx. And who knows what else may have gotten out over the years that he didn't tell anyone about. A zookeeper can be fired if a dangerous animal gets out by his error, especially if incidents happen more than one time. But somehow Zeke still had his job. He wasn't really careless so much as had a tendency to be lazy. Sometimes he took unwise shortcuts, or just seemed to always have unusual things happen to him. He was one of the original keepers when the zoo opened and felt devoted to its success.

Zeke's most notorious incident, by far, occurred when he made a crucial error with the orangutans. It happened coincidentally on the very day that the recently hired zoo director started work—not a good way to impress the new head honcho. The opening hour of the zoo had to be delayed most of the day until the prickly predicament was resolved.

At the orangutan exhibit the keeper can choose from two different doors to move from his work area where the animals' indoor enclosures are to the outside exhibit. To shift the orangs from the inside quarters out to the exhibit the keeper operates orangutan-sized hydraulic doors that give them access to a transfer "tunnel" made of hefty mesh. Four orangs lived at the zoo at the time: "Bo," the big male; "Tiddlywink," a 6-year-old female; and

12-year-old "Myrna" with her new baby "Frodo." A full-grown and obese adult male, Bo stood only about 4 1/2 feet tall. Because in the wild they live in trees, orangutans have the greatest arm strength of all the primates, stronger even than gorillas, which explains why powerful hydraulic doors are necessary to shift them on and off exhibit. Orangs naturally live a mostly solitary existence, so to protect the baby we would put Bo out on display by himself at a different time from the other three…sometimes Bo could be a real grouch. So here's what happened.

The day started the usual way with Zeke preparing the exhibit while the orangs waited in their night quarters. He entered from the keeper area by one door, leaving it open—a grave error. After he cleaned and then distributed palm fronds, burlap sacks, and the food, he left the exhibit by the second keeper door and locked it behind him. But he had completely forgotten that he had left that first door open. Fortunately for Zeke, only one orang was going on display that morning. Unfortunately, that orang was Bo.

Without checking both keeper doors first as he should, thinking all was secure, Zeke opened Bo's hydraulic door to let him out to the exhibit. A moment later as Zeke came back around to the other side of the keeper area to work in the kitchen, there stood Bo's enormous, imposing form, silhouetted in the open keeper doorway. Zeke shuddered in fear and disbelief. He happened to be pushing a wheelbarrow full of fresh hay bedding, so as Bo ominously shuffled straight toward him he gave it a good shove in the orang's direction. Then Zeke bolted for the outside double doors, slamming them shut behind him. Shut, but not locked!

To his great dismay, the keeper realized that his keys still hung in the lock (another critical error), on the inside of the door that he now pressed against with all his weight and muscle. He could feel his blood coursing through his temples. Zeke's knees sagged as he heard the orang sniffing and grunting just on the other side of the door from him. And he could see a sliver of Bo's inquisitive brown eye peering through the crack between the doors.

If the orang had thought to try pushing on them, Zeke wouldn't have had a chance at stopping Bo's 250 lbs. from going through these outside doors the keeper so desperately mashed himself against. But with all the neat stuff inside the keeper work area that Bo could always only see—and now had access to—he soon lost all interest in the doors. Astonished by the prospect of

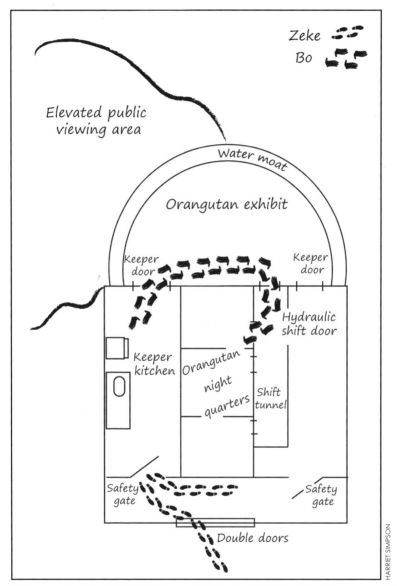

Zeke

Bo

Elevated public viewing area

Water moat

Orangutan exhibit

Keeper door

Keeper door

Hydraulic shift door

Keeper kitchen

Orangutan night quarters

Shift tunnel

Safety gate

Safety gate

Double doors

HARRIET SIMPSON

this new adventure he didn't know what to do first. The night house wasn't visible to the public so it was nothing special in appearance, just utilitarian. The electrical conduit and plumbing pipes clung to the naked concrete block walls in plain view. All those intriguing aluminum and copper pipes

DICK GEORGE

Bornean orangutan

snaking up the wall looked irresistible, and Bo ripped them apart like they were paper straws. Thoroughly absorbed in his project, the drenching shower Bo received from one of the mangled pipes didn't faze him a bit.

Meanwhile, Zeke took advantage of Bo's diverted attention. With hands shaking and heart pounding, he cautiously opened the door a crack. He snuck inside to retrieve his keys from the lock and then ducked back out, securing the doors from outside. Concerned that exposed wiring and spurting water from the crumpled pipes might electrocute Bo, Zeke tripped the circuit breakers and shut off the water supply (lucky for him, the controls for both were located outside the building). Now, though, how to get that pesky ape back into his night quarters without putting any keepers or the animal at risk?

Realizing he was unable to resolve the situation on his own, Zeke, sweating profusely, sprinted to the main office. First he had the secretary alert the security staff to delay the opening of the zoo (luckily it was still early so no visitors had come onto the grounds yet). Then he notified the curator and veterinarian, who dropped everything to assemble a crew of additional keepers. They all rendezvoused at the exhibit and concocted various strategies to resolve this unique dilemma.

In the meantime, over the next few hours Bo merrily and methodically peeled Formica from the countertops, yanked the sink and cabinets off the wall, turned the refrigerator into a great pile of unrecognizable pieces, chewed the hoses into rubbery chunks, and destroyed anything and everything else that he could get to. He totally demolished the place.

Standing outside in the public viewing area, keepers yelled, banged on buckets, whistled, and generally tried anything and everything to divert Bo away from his fanatical demolition work. Some stationed themselves at strategic locations with radios, monitoring his activities as best they could and still be safe. It took three long hours to entice Bo to abandon his frolic and move outside. When he finally appeared, the reptile keepers stood ready for him.

In the past, a keeper witnessed an instance when a wild snake inadvertently ventured into the orangutan exhibit. Bo, it turns out, is terrified of snakes. Actually, Myrna is too, but she had stood her ground that day, flailing away at the snake with a palm frond. Big strong Bo, on the other hand, had escaped for where he felt the most secure, which, a lucky omen for Zeke, was his night house.

The keepers placed their biggest python in a sling attached to a jury-rigged extension pole. They gently lowered it down the 20 feet from the elevated viewing area right into the water of the exhibit moat. As the 15-foot-long snake swam toward land, which also happened to be straight at the orang, Bo couldn't flee fast enough to the mesh tunnel leading back to the safety of his night quarters. An alerted keeper tiptoed in and shut the hydraulic door (fortunately on a separate electrical circuit) immediately behind him. I wonder who felt more relieved—Bo or the keepers....

Several days of labor and considerable expense returned the night house to a functional level after Bo's extensive remodeling efforts. And somehow, astonishingly, Zeke still managed to retain his job. If things had turned out differently, with an orangutan or people getting seriously hurt, he surely would have been fired. Maybe the director simply didn't want to have to discharge someone his first day on the job.

———

By now you may have noticed that several of the zoo's worst incidents involved the awesome and cunning male orangutan Bo. Each orang has its own distinct personality, but generally speaking they are not blatantly aggressive. In fact they're usually quite passive. They just have an incredible potential for danger because of their size, extraordinary strength, intelligence, and surprising speed. Most of the keepers who worked with Bo for any length of time considered this imposing creature the most dangerous of all at this zoo. He made such enduring impressions that even years after not working with him anymore, keepers confess to having frequent 'Bo dreams.' Or more aptly, Bo nightmares.

It is thankfully rare, but a few zoo visitors seem to have an insatiable desire to throw food, rocks, garbage, or other foreign objects into exhibits, or even maliciously at the animals to goad them into reacting. In years past, many zoos (including ours) allowed the public to feed their animals. Persistent pleas from keepers convinced management that marshmallows, heavily salted popcorn, and other junk food were just not sensible, which finally led to a ban on public feeding. This also enabled keepers to intercept anyone observed throwing anything into an exhibit. But people persist in wanting a way to personally connect with animals. Even prominently displayed warning signs not to throw things are sometimes deliberately ignored.

Tragically, Bo became a victim of this frustrating aspect of zoos. With a "laid back" personality it's not always easy to tell when an orangutan isn't feeling well. For a couple of days Bo acted a bit more tranquil than normal and had an unusual diminished appetite, which the keepers noted on their daily reports. On the third morning they were stunned to find Bo dead.

The veterinarian performed a necropsy (animal autopsy), which is standard protocol at zoos. She discovered a tight, decomposing wad of rubber strands that had caused blockage and a subsequent infection in Bo's digestive system. Someone had thrown a golf ball into the exhibit, which in innocence Bo eagerly identified as an unusual treat to be consumed.

Although the source of anxiety at work and in our dreams, Bo was an extraordinary animal that we all loved. He had the impressive fleshy cheek pads and big throat sac characteristic of a full adult male. I can't convey to you how awesome it felt to admire his coarse skin and tangled orange hair while he looked straight into your eyes from just inches away. His senseless passing was appalling and exceedingly difficult for the community and all the zoo employees to endure. What an inane death for such a magnificent creature.

The King and I

Unique situations, incredible opportunities, and potential dangers…a zookeeper can't help but collect potent lifelong memories when working with animals. Any keeper can explicitly relate the most memorable moments of his or her career, and I can certainly tell you mine. But usually the description only hints at the true intensity of the sensations and emotions of the experience. Here's the story at the top of my memory list.

In the wild, an animal's poor health or a debilitating physical condition means a natural death sentence, but those living in captivity often set longevity records. Our male African lion, Imara, had lived well past the average 15-year lifespan of a wild one. He was so old that many of his teeth were gone, he limped with crippling arthritis, and cataracts clouded his eyes. He still had a good appetite but began to look emaciated, so he probably suffered other health issues typical of old felines such as kidney disease, diabetes, or thyroid problems. Imara's quality of life had deteriorated to the point that the zoo director, mammal curator, and veterinarian reluctantly concurred that the time had come. It would be most humane to euthanize him. His loss was sure going to be hard on zoo staff and patrons since he had lived here a long 30 years, and was among the first animals the zoo acquired.

So on that fateful sad morning the vet called me on the radio, asking to meet him at the lion exhibit. I backed the truck up to the service door and dropped the tailgate, then lugged in the big canvas tarp. The vet had already administered the compassionate shot and Imara lay lifeless on the floor of his sleeping quarters.

I stood wondering what would be the best way to handle this with just the two of us. After spreading the tarp and tucking it the length of the lion's back, I sat down and, for leverage, snuggled up as close to Imara as I could. As we prepared to roll his limp 500-pound body onto the tarp I wrapped my arms around this magnificent animal's head, cradling him next to my chest. With his enormous head completely filling my arms his face loomed right next to mine. I savored the privilege of being able to admire this majestic beast for the last time, more intimately than I ever could have imagined. Imara's thick coarse hair all brown and curly with gleaming red and gold highlights looked stunning, and as good a mane as an adult male lion gets. And with my face just inches away, the distinctive smell of his oily locks permeated my nose.

As his still-warm head rested on my lap I reached across his neck to pull on his front leg while the vet grasped his hind legs. My hand couldn't even span half way around Imara's leg, so I grabbed a handful of the characteristically long tufts of black hair that grew on the side of his knee. He was so heavy I couldn't even budge him. We tugged, trying to get the impossible momentum of his dead weight going. As his body finally began to roll, I heard a rumbling gurgle of air leaving the lion's lungs.

That must be what's called the "death rattle," I thought to myself. I've always wondered what that sounded like.

At the same instant I noticed a protracted blink as his milky right eye seemed to look directly at me.

Must be just an after-death nerve twitch, I told myself.

Then the lion's upper lip slowly contracted up into a snarl, exposing an enormous yellowed canine tooth with its jagged rim of brown tartar. He gurgled again. And from his toes, just inches from my hand, thick yellow claws slowly extended and retracted, and extended and retracted again. It felt like forever, but just a split second of time passed between Imara's growling grimace and my realization of the danger the vet and I now faced.

I screamed, "He's not dead!" and instantly freed myself from the embrace. My body seemed to defy the laws of physics as I somehow jerked

DICK HILTON

my legs out from under the lion and stumbled to my feet. I felt like a marionette. One very lucky marionette.

One difficult aspect of an exotic animal veterinarian's job is that he sometimes has to guess an animal's weight to calculate the ideal dosage of a tranquilizer or other drugs. In this case, Imara needed just a little bit more of the euthanizing drug than he administered. It would have helped if the vet had remembered to bring the stethoscope to check his heartbeat, too, before we got so intimate with his body.

As happens with many people after a traumatic incident I have little memory of what happened immediately after that stark, terrifying moment, but it doesn't matter since no further drama occurred. But all the sights, sounds, textures, smells, and emotions of that incident so many years ago feel nearly as vivid today as on that morning. After all was over, I roamed about the zoo for a good long time waiting for the adrenalin effects to wear off. Meanwhile I contemplated the high of the honor I felt embracing Imara's regal head versus the sheer terror imagining the "what if" as so often comes to a keeper's mind.

Can you guess what this creature might be...

Epilogue: Still Want To?

Some tips for prospective zookeepers

Are you hoping to be an animal keeper one day? If reading this book didn't change your mind, may I offer a bit of advice? First and foremost, GET THAT EDUCATION! Nowadays, most zoos (especially the larger ones) require a college degree. And EXPERIENCE working directly with animals is a must. It is not enough to just "love animals." How about working for a local veterinarian while attending college to get hands-on experience? If you can afford it, maybe volunteer at the zoo while awaiting that zoo job opening. You've got to show prospective employers that you are serious about your aspirations.

Two professional organizations offer membership even if you are not a zoo employee. AZA is the American Association of Zoos and Aquariums (aza.org) and AAZK is the American Association of Zoo Keepers (aazk.org). At the least check out their web pages. You can access a lot of interesting information on the sites without having to be a member, such as: zoo and world conservation issues; announcements of conferences at various locations across the country; links to research and other animal-related job sites; and, yippee!—zoo internship and job listings. Two of the perks of belonging to AZA or AAZK include an entrance fee discount at member zoos and reduced rates to attend their conferences. Besides hearing about the latest zoo developments, the stimulating meetings at these conferences provide unique opportunities to meet people in the field and do some networking. You know, the old "it's not what you know it's who you know." That can often be the key to landing a job.

You may be more likely to have a shot at employment at a small zoo. Personally I think they are more fun to work at anyway as they have more of a "family operation" atmosphere. You feel like you are a part of the zoo's total activities and get to know more of your coworkers better rather than doing a monotonous job in a single area of a big zoo with little chance for deviation.

If you are actively seeking a job don't let your application languish in a zoo office filing cabinet. Positions don't become available very often, so keep in touch periodically to let them know that you are still interested and available. Familiarize yourself with the zoo's layout and collection, and maybe even introduce yourself to keepers and to the curators who do the hiring (but don't be a pest either!). Then as you become a familiar face they may begin to think of you as a potential coworker.

Some keepers get their start by first working in a section other than the animal department, and there are many opportunities: horticulture, security, concessions, education, maintenance, administration, or the medical center. This way you can be among the first to be aware of an opening and you will have proven that you have what it takes to be a keeper—capable, hardworking, sensible, and dependable.

Some zoos prepare keepers in their own training programs or have internships (these may mean working for low or no pay). Another alternative could be college courses. At least two community colleges offer specific zoo-related degrees where you can attain

...it's a white pelican!

DICK HILTON

education and experience at the same time. At Santa Fe Community College in Gainesville, FL, students get practical experience at a small zoo right on the campus while enrolled in related courses. Moorpark College in Ventura, CA, offers studies geared more toward animal training. Check the AAZK site for more information.

Teach yourself as well, READ! And read some more! Frequent libraries and choose from the plethora of magazines and books on animals and nature. Your local library may have *The International Zoo Yearbook*, an outstanding set of books covering a complete range of zoo topics. Or look it up on the Internet for some fascinating reading.

Good luck job-hunting, and when successful, I hope you enjoy your career as much as I did. Have fun and STAY SAFE!!

DICK GEORGE

Simply reacting to an annoying fly, this longhorn steer could impale a keeper with an innocent, unexpected toss of his head.

This rhino's mother was old and nearly blind, but consistently fantastic at parenting. The week-old calf always kept close to her side, til one day mom accidentally stepped on one of his feet, breaking his leg. How would you like to have been the zoo veterinarian that day?

Appendix

What Goes On In There?

Have you ever asked yourself, "Just what does a zookeeper do all day?" Or noticed a person in uniform disappear into the lion exhibit and wonder, What if something were to go drastically wrong? This section gives a basic overview of the day-to-day of what a keeper's job is like, so it may be a bit dry for someone not intent on a career working with animals. It is brief out of necessity, and some parts may repeat elements mentioned in the preceding tales. And because each zoo has its own particular jargon and ways of doing things, I won't bother to try to cover those variables.

The Basics

Everyone knows that the fundamental part of a zookeeper's job is to provide food, water, and clean living quarters for the animals under their care, and of course occasional medical needs. It sounds simple, but it's a lot of hard work and a sobering responsibility; being captive, these animals are wholly dependent on you for their quality of life. Besides the essentials there is often a much longer list of chores. Most have to be done every day or a couple of times a week, others just once in a while.

Nothing is truly typical or average about a day when you're working with live animals, but there are basic routines that keepers follow to get their work done: read daily activity reports, check animals, feed and clean, and at the end of the day check animals again and fill out a report. Sticking to a routine prevents keepers from forgetting the many details they deal with, like being sure to secure every one of the endless number of locks opened throughout each day. The animals also become accustomed to the time schedule, and some may even become upset or suspicious when a routine is changed. Keepers have an early start to their workday because there's so much to get done before the zoo opens for visitors, which often means starting work just as the sun is rising.

A keeper's workload is commonly referred to as something like an area, string or section. Depending on the total number of animals, types of exhibits, and number of keepers, these sections can vary widely in size and composition. Sections are arranged so that each keeper is responsible for roughly the same amount of daily work. For example, maintaining five aviaries that are 20'x20'x15' with a total of sixteen birds of six types would take more time than one 50'x80' pen with a pair of zebras, which takes longer than eight 3'x5'x3' reptile displays with twelve snakes.

Conditions can obviously vary, but in general zoos in colder climates have more indoor exhibits inside buildings, while those in moderate climates can display most animals outdoors. If all the reptile exhibits are housed in one building, the keeper may spend the entire day working there, while a

bird keeper's aviaries can be scattered throughout the zoo. It's then more efficient to have a vehicle like a golf cart for transporting the wide variety of necessary equipment, such as: rake, toolbox, shovel, trash bucket, deck broom, hose, a variety of nets, etc. A bird keeper also hauls buckets of different kinds of food like parrot seed mix, monkey biscuits, turkey crumbles, nuts, and dog chow kibbles. Then there are the pans of chopped fruits and vegetables, hard-boiled eggs, meats, crickets, and mealworms to deliver.

Every exhibit's food containers need to be kept clean and stocked. And, of course, by feeding the animals, there is a need for cleaning up the "end results" as well. Ponds or water bowls are scrubbed and exhibit areas raked.

The displays' appearances are spiffed up as needed, which may include replacing trampled or eaten plants, or hauling in soil to restore what's been gradually depleted with daily raking. In addition to the displays themselves, keepers may sometimes be responsible for maintaining the appearance of the area where the public stands to view the animals. There is a regular, thorough check of exhibit condition. Are the fences and gates secure? Have any animals (from inside or out) dug a hole under the fence? Is there damage from vandalism? Do climbing structures, perches or ropes need repair? Then there are seasonal adjustments like putting up shade screen to block the baking sun, or installing a heat lamp in frigid weather.

Categories

The Animal Departments of most zoos may have special work categories. An evening keeper drives around the grounds after the day keepers have left for the day, to check one last time that all is well, bring animals into their night quarters once the zoo closes, give final feedings and medications, etc. A relief keeper, trained in several different sections, fills in for regular keepers during illness, holidays or vacation.

In addition to assisting the veterinarian, the keepers at the zoo's medical facility perform the usual basic feeding and cleaning duties for any patients. But they have the added challenges of a constantly changing assortment of creatures, with myriads of medical problems and special care needs.

At some zoos, each keeper prepares the foods and cleans dishes for the animals in their care. At other institutions a commissary keeper not only prepares a vast variety of diets for many of the animals (starting at an ungodly early hour), but also keeps the kitchen stocked with plenty of fresh produce and eggs, sacks and hoppers full of seeds and feeds, and the freezer full of meats and fish. At the end of the day this keeper cleans the floors, countertops, food processors and other equipment, and runs mountains of dishes through the industrial dishwasher.

Sometimes animals' diets are prepared the day previous to delivery and stored in a refrigerator big enough to walk in. Selections are made from a wide variety of fruits and vegetables and chopped according to the needs of the animals—like chunks for parrots and primates, or minced bits for small birds and tortoises. Fish and meat for the carnivores must be weighed out in specific amounts so that they are fed just the right amount—too much food

DICK GEORGE

and a less active life style quickly result in obesity problems. The diets are prepared according to each animal's or exhibit's own menu card.

The Workday

A keeper's workday begins by reading over the previous day's "Daily Activity Report" of events such as births, deaths, transfers, medical notes, maintenance needs, observations, etc., in his or her particular section and perhaps the zoo in general. At the end of the work shift, each keeper fills out their own report, noting everything that happened in their section. These are left for the evening keeper and next day's keepers to read. Copies of the reports are passed on to the medical staff and to a record-keeper, known as a registrar, so that the information can be entered into each animal's permanent records. You'd be amazed at the exceptional detail of the records maintained on most every specimen in a zoo's collection.

Animals are amazingly adaptive, readily falling into the daily zoo routine. With a reward of food, those considered particularly dangerous are persuaded to come inside to their night quarters. Topping that list are elephants, great apes, and big cats. In addition to safety, having the animals conditioned is also more efficient. With the animals inside for the night, the first thing the next morning the keeper can clean and prepare the empty exhibits, then shift the animals to their displays. Later, after all the animals are on exhibit and the zoo is open, the keeper returns to clean the night quarters. These indoor holding areas also come in handy when animals need to be kept inside during illness, bad weather, construction, while giving birth, or when a newcomer is being gradually introduced to the exhibit, cohabitants, and routine.

Broken Routine

Often the keeper's daily routine is broken when unexpected things happen like vandalism, a medical emergency, or a spurting water pipe. The infinite variety of challenges is limitless, including such possibilities as: being available for sixteen feedings spread throughout the day when hand-raising orphaned toucan chicks; attending a design meeting for a new hippo exhibit; assisting in stitching up a capuchin monkey injured in a fight; giving a private tour of the elephant facility to potential donors; clipping a crowned pigeon's overgrown toenails; or shipping a pair of spider monkeys to another zoo. Big deal, you might think. Some of these don't seem like they'd be much to cope with. But let's take a closer look at the shipping example to see just what may be involved.

Let's say that your zoo has a pair of spider monkeys available to loan to another zoo, and one in Chicago calls to say they're interested. The following is the sequence of activities over a lengthy period of time needed to get the animals relocated:

1 – Find out what general date Chicago wants the monkeys shipped, bearing in mind the severe limits of weather extremes.

2 – Inquire as to when Chicago's quarantine facility will have space open. (All newly acquired animals are kept separate from the rest of a zoo's collection for at least a month to ensure they are healthy.)

3 – Well in advance, because government bureaucracy can sometimes take a while, have the registrar apply for any federal or state permits needed to accompany the shipment. This gets especially complicated with endangered species.

4 – Notify the veterinarian so the animals can be examined for a health certificate required by the airlines, and research if any vaccinations are needed to cross state lines.

5 – Submit a request to the maintenance department for the construction

of two shipping crates to particular mandated specifications of materials, size, doors, windows and flooring.

6 – Call several different airlines to find the most direct flight and best shipping times to minimize the animals' transit time.

7 – Relay that information to Chicago to verify that it works for them.

8 – Request the registrar to copy the monkeys' records to accompany the shipment.

9 – Arrange for contracts to be issued with the loan agreement details.

10 – Reserve a zoo vehicle to transport the crates to airfreight on shipping day.

11 – Write up address and information labels and affix to the crates.

12 – Securely fasten empty food and water containers and install bedding in the crates.

13 – On shipping day, juicy foods and water go into the containers.

14 – Getting the monkeys safely into the crates is then the truly challenging part.

15 – Transport the animals to the airline's airfreight office.

16 – On return from the airport, notify Chicago that the animals are en route.

17 – Record the transfer on the daily keeper report. Then hopefully the Chicago zoo will notify you of the animals' safe arrival.

See what I mean? And I've undoubtedly left something out somewhere along the line.

Control of vermin or other unwanted intruders is a constant battle at zoos that can cut into a keeper's work time significantly. Most are freeloaders helping themselves to someone else's meal. Aside from costing the zoo a lot of money in pilfered feed, there is also the risk of disease being spread to the valuable exhibit specimens. And some vermin are potential predators to exhibit animals. Depending on the zoo's location, the list of unwanted possible interlopers can be surprisingly long. Not just the obvious mice, pigeons, and cockroaches, but also rats, cats, dogs, house (aka English) sparrows, mallards, Canada geese, European starlings, gulls, coyotes, hawks, owls, snakes, squirrels, foxes, raccoons, skunks, and the ubiquitous ants. Instituting control methods for even just a couple of these troublemakers can be very time consuming.

Obviously an animal escape is not routine, and fortunately a pretty rare occurrence. An unwritten rule intimates that as long as the animal remains nearby, there's a chance it can be wangled back into the exhibit. Usually. If you're really lucky. That enclosure has become the animal's territory, and it feels safe there. Once out in an unfamiliar area, if offered an open door and sometimes the mate or roommates in sight, an escapee is usually more than anxious to return on its own. More often, the strategy can get more complicated, and unfortunately, sometimes much more dangerous.

Reproduction

Riding high on the wave of the conservation movement of the 1970s, zoos began to concentrate on maintaining pairs or groups of animals and working out their requirements for successful reproduction. The various needs can be as basic as quiet privacy to providing particular elements such as a nest cavity or den, bedding or nest material, diet supplements, or lights on timers to simulate a longer day. Captive reproduction has been successful in all but a few animals, eliminating or reducing the need for collecting from the wild. Some, like cheetahs and pandas, have been particularly challenging. Zoos across the country and around the world are in constant communication with each other, sharing information and their animals through sale, trade or loan.

The plastron of the male desert tortoise is concave to accommodate the female's carapace during breeding; her plastron is flat.

Most people might be surprised to learn that with certain captive animals reproduction has become so successful, in fact, that many species (most notably primates and the large cats) are on some form of birth control to prevent overpopulation in zoos. After all, there's a limit to just how many animals can be housed at each facility. Ironically, reproduction may have to be curtailed even for endangered species, as one of the ideal goals—returning them to the wild—is not always possible. This is because their habitat has been taken over by humans, or they can't survive because of the introduction of non-native animals. A good example is the Nene goose, nearly annihilated in its native Hawaii by the predatory mongoose, pig, rat, cat, and dog, all brought to the islands by humans.

Creativity

One of the more creative parts of a keeper's job is devising "behavioral enrichments." These are simply changes in an animal's captive environment that allow it to perform natural behaviors for mental and physical activity or comfort, such as foraging for food, climbing, gnawing on wood, or bathing in a mud hole. This may be as easy as providing a log for a bobcat to scratch, or more challenging like designing a complicated and indestructible food dispenser for a bear to prolong and challenge the feeding routine (while hopefully not adding significantly to a keeper's workload).

Zoo employees often attend conferences, which cover a myriad of topics where zoo professionals share diverse information and ideas, resulting in explosive changes like the following few examples:

-Architectural features such as moats or islands and natural looking exhibits to replace bars and concrete floors;

-Duplication of habitat (challenging, but these innovations provide mental and physical comfort for the animals, and infinitely more appeal to the zoo visitor. Many facilities try to immerse their visitors in the habitat of the animals they're viewing too, a pleasant and educational experience.);

-Extensive graphics and educational programs that enlighten the community;

- Behavioral enrichment ideas are communicated, sharing creative brainstorming about what works—and what doesn't—in this imaginative and challenging field. The high priorities of conservation, education, and esthetics reflect vast progress at today's zoological gardens.

One Extreme To Another

Who becomes an animal keeper? And what reason do they give for wanting to? Most often the phrase "I love animals" passes the lips of a prospective keeper. I wish I had a nickel for every time I've heard it when interviewing candidates or chatting with dreamy-eyed zoo visitors. To the employer, however, that reason can be a red flag. Inexperienced animal lovers may not be aware of just how much hard, dirty work is involved in being an animal keeper. Not to mention the potential for heartaches from harsh reality when the animal that you've worked with closely for years gets shipped to another zoo. Or worse, gets ill or dies.

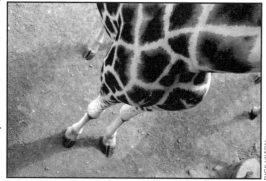

At the other extreme, a prospective keeper that since childhood has kept his own little menageries of chickens, rabbits, snakes or other pets has plenty of realistic experience but could prove troublesome to work with. He may have what might be considered bad habits, such as lower standards of cleanliness that can be difficult for that person to raise to the level the zoo and the public expects. *

Childhood animal maintainers might also be cocky and a bit blasé when it comes to safety. Working with venomous snakes for instance. A green keeper is trained to observe a variety of safety procedures when reaching into a reptile exhibit. Someone who has maintained his own collection of rattlesnakes can be a valuable employee with experience and intuition. He has learned how to read an animal's behavior over the years, and may think he can avoid being injured without taking the effort to use the usual safeguards. And most times he can. But being too lazy to take proper precautions is just not acceptable.

Please bear in mind that most all the stories in this book took place at a time where there was little funding for a young, developing facility, and we certainly didn't have the luxury of cell phones back then (can you even imagine that?!). Times have changed exponentially in regard to safety and communication, so incidents today truly are exceedingly rare.

Now that you've got a good idea what the job is like I hope I may have helped inspire you to pursue your dream....

DICK GEORGE

About the Author

During her eighteen-year career as a zookeeper and curator of birds, Kristin compiled true behind-the-scenes experiences from three different zoos that give the reader insight into a zookeeper's job. She lives with her husband, Dick (a geology professor/paleontologist), and two cats in the beautiful northern California foothills of the Sierra Nevada Mountains.

Visit www.zoogoofsbook.com
For information please email info@zoogoofsbook.com

DICK GEORGE

KRISTIN HILTON